Connection:

Understanding Our Mormon Friends and Neighbors

Rodger S. Russell

© 2015

by Rodger Russell

All rights reserved

Printed in the United States of America

Thirteen-digit ISBN 978-1511766456
Ten-digit ISBN 15117665X

Front Cover Photo credit, Susan Chiang
Back Cover Photo credit, Nathan Russell Photography

All Scripture quotations are King James Version

To all my Mormon friends and neighbors, we "other" Christians just want to understand you, your church, and your beliefs. May these words facilitate the dialogue.

And

To the members, past and present of Holladay Baptist Church (Now Risen Life Church) in Salt Lake City, Utah where the material for this book was developed and well received.

Contents

Preface . . . . **vii**

Introduction Why Write This Book? 8

1. **Revelation** How Do We Know Anything About God? 11
2. **The Book of Mormon** Another Testament of Jesus Christ 25
3. **Other LDS Scripture** Joseph Smith as a Prophet and Translator 41
4. **Who Is God?** Is He an exalted Man? 50
5. **Who is Jesus Christ?** The Son of God, or A Son of God? . 62
6. **Salvation and The Gospel** How Do We Become Right With God? 72
7. **Humankind** Who Am I and Where Did I come From? 81
8. **Temples and Ordinances** Does God Live in A House? . . .89
9. **The Priesthood** Where Do You Get Authority? 98

Appendices

I. A Short history of Mormonism 103
II. Requirements for Exaltation. 106
III. The Organization of the Church. 108
IV. The Adam God Doctrine. 110
V. The Joseph Smith Translation of the Bible. 113
VI. Mormons and Polygamy 114
VII. The Mormon View of Heaven 116

Endnotes 118

vi

PREFACE

My LDS friends need to know that in the title and throughout the book I have used the word Mormon often. I know Mormon is not the preferred title for the Church of Jesus Christ of Latter Day Saints. I am aware that on some level you believe it is a derisive name and not the official name of the church. I have chosen to use it in the title based on the familiarity of the term with my target readers. The full title, The Church of Jesus Christ of Latter Day Saints, is cumbersome. Historically, not every church has been able to choose the name by which it is called. Baptist began as a derisive name for the re-baptizers of the sixteenth and seventeenth centuries.

I am also aware that most of you think we are out of line for talking about what you believe. We study your beliefs because you first challenged us to read the Book of Mormon. Your claims for that Book, and the church that followed its publication, is something we do not accept by blind faith. We accept the challenge of scripture to "Prove all things" (1 Thessalonians 5:21 KJV).

I want to be fair to your beliefs. If I have misrepresented your beliefs in some way, it is unintentional. I have had numerous discussions with my own friends and neighbors, as well as LDS missionaries both in my home and at LDS church sites. I have read books written by LDS authorities, BYU professors, and other apologists for the LDS faith. I have a library of books by LDS authors that I have purchased from Deseret Books, and I have read many issues of *Ensign* magazine. I have attended the local ward and listened to talks, and I have read countless LDS speeches and papers that have been given to me by LDS friends. You probably do not know me, but my intention is to present Mormonism clearly and without distortion so my Evangelical friends can understand you better.

To my Evangelical friends. The material in this book does not come from anti-Mormon sources. I purposely mainly used LDS sources in my research, and the material about Mormonism is from current LDS material. After twenty-four years in Utah, however, I have read a lot of those anti-Mormon materials, and there may be some residual thought or material from some of them. The basis for this book is a class I taught on Wednesday nights in Salt Lake City that was attended by both my congregation and some of their LDS friends and neighbors.

Evangelicals, you may have read a lot of negative material directed toward the LDS Church. My purpose is not to demonize the church, but to encourage dialogue between you and your LDS co-workers and friends. It is difficult to have a discussion with someone when you insist they believe something they do not believe or they do not know it is a teaching of the church.

My prayer for this work is simple: "Lord, help it clear the way for meaningful conversation."

Dr. Rodger S. Russell

Salt Lake City, April, 2012

INTRODUCTION

Why Write This Book?

Why do we need another book on Mormonism? Twenty-three years as the pastor of three Baptist Churches in Utah have convinced me that there is a significant difference between the doctrines non-Mormons have been taught that Mormons believe and the actual beliefs of our Mormon friends and neighbors. Many evangelical works have been written to explain the teachings of Mormonism. They can be found in any Christian bookstore. They are helpful to non-Mormons for understanding the historical teachings of the LDS church and the teachings of Joseph Smith, Brigham Young, and the line of Prophets who have followed them.

Well-meaning cult experts explain these historical teachings and present them to us as Mormon doctrine. Then, thinking we are well armed, we set out to talk to our Mormon friends and neighbors. Many times we discover that they don't believe some of the stranger doctrines. They have never even heard of them. The only avenue left to us is to try to teach them what their Church really believes. Yes, it is as absurd as it sounds.

My purpose in writing this book is to help my readers understand the beliefs of our Mormon friends and neighbors. My desire is to help others see how Mormon beliefs differ from Evangelical Christian theology. I have no intention of ridiculing in any way the LDS church or our LDS friends. While I find many of their doctrines and teachings to be strange, my intent is not to make light of their devoutly held beliefs. At the same time, attempts to redefine Mormonism as a mainstream Christian denomination need to be addressed. Mormonism is not orthodox Christianity, even if orthodoxy is defined loosely.

We should not be surprised if our Mormon friends will not accept this book. They may be somewhat offended that we would attempt to examine their beliefs at such a detailed level. Many of them honestly do not understand why we are interested in their teachings. They wish we wouldn't discuss the differences.

This is not a work entitled "How to Witness to your LDS Friends and Neighbors." While I pray the result of understanding is evangelism, this book is not a how to manual. The purpose of this work is to try to understand the actual beliefs of the Mormons we are most likely to meet and to compare them with evangelical beliefs.

I am also aware that there is no "one" Mormon belief. Mormons take free agency very literally, and to varying degrees they feel at liberty to disagree with one another. Just as each Christian believes a little, or sometimes a lot, differently from other Christians, so LDS church members are not all of one mind on many subjects. This book can only be a guideline to understanding our LDS friends. To understand them we will have to engage them in conversation. I hope to inspire that conversation as well as to give the confidence needed to engage them. My desire is for Evangelical Christians to become comfortable with three things: 1) accepting their own doctrinal beliefs, 2) giving an account for their hope in Christ, 3) speaking of these things with friends and neighbors.

As we focus on Mormon beliefs, the subject is not about what Brigham Young preached. The same is true for Joseph Smith. While the average LDS member would tell us differently, thinking Mormons know they do not believe everything these former prophets taught nor do they accept them as authoritative for today. This causes no small misunderstanding.

The sources I have used for the LDS beliefs in this work are mostly LDS. Most of them are very modern sources. These are books that can be purchased at any Deseret Book Store as well as at many Wal-Mart stores in Utah. They are written for the use of today's LDS person. In addition, I will draw upon the many discussions, debates, and yes, arguments I have had over the years with missionaries, members, and ex-members of the LDS church.

As I examine LDS scripture, I will consider what our LDS friends are being taught today. I will compare their beliefs to my own Evangelical Christian Theology and discuss the differences. It should not be surprising that there are significant differences. Most Christians and their LDS friends understand that they have different beliefs. Materials printed by the LDS Church declare that they have different beliefs from non-Mormons. B. H. Roberts, an LDS theologian from the first part of the 20th century, says, "It is very easily proved that we have differences. They don't need proofs that we have differences. We will concede that. Mormons not only admit the variances, but glory in them."[1] Mormons know that other faith systems believe different things, and they are happy to admit it.

Robert Millet is a professor at Brigham Young University, the flagship school of the LDS church. The second appendix in his book *The Mormon Faith: A New Look at Christianity* is entitled "Distinctive LDS doctrines." He mentions three teachings that "other Christians" (his words) do not believe. The doctrines he mentions are LDS teachings about God and man, the pre-mortal existence of man, and baptism for the dead.[2] These doctrines will be a part of this discussion.

I do not claim to be an expert in the history and documents of Mormonism. Many others are more qualified to teach "Mormonism." My perspective is that of a pastor. I want to help evangelicals become more comfortable with their own faith as we deal with those around us who are LDS. We need to be able to give an account for the hope that is in us in Jesus Christ.

1
Revelation

How Do We Know Anything About God?

I was coaching youth baseball when an incident arose that called for the coach to approach the umpire about a rule that was being broken. I called time out and presented the rule to the umpire. He pulled out his rulebook and did a quick search and then showed me that my understanding of the rule was incorrect. Since I did not have my rulebook with me, I had to accept his ruling. After all, he showed me in his book that I was incorrect. Later, at home, I got out my rulebook and looked the rule up. What I discovered was that there was a different rule in place, depending on the age of the players. I was looking at the rules for ages 13-15, which was the age I was coaching. The umpire showed me the rule for ages 16-18.

It is difficult to play the game by the rules when they come in different rulebooks. We face this same difficulty when we begin to discuss matters of faith with our Mormon friends and neighbors. We live by different guidebooks.

An understanding of any religion begins with revelation. A simple definition of revelation is the way God has revealed his presence, activities, and will to humankind. General revelation is how God reveals his existence and a little of what He is like to all people at all times. The Psalmist describes this kind of revelation: "The heavens declare the glory of God, and the firmament showeth his handiwork" (Psalm 19:1).

Conversation with our Mormon friends will quickly confirm that our belief in general revelation is very similar to theirs. Where our guidebooks diverge is at the point of special revelation. Special revelation is the unveiling of God's plan for the world. Special revelation tells how we can have a relationship with the creator. It gives us necessary information on what God expects and how we can live to please Him.

For the evangelical, special revelation means the word of God, both written and in the flesh. The written word of God is the Old Testament and the New Testament. The word in the

5

flesh is Jesus Christ. For our LDS neighbor, however, there is more. They have a different guidebook. The only way to understand our Mormon neighbors is by understanding their guidebook.

Scripture

While evangelicals believe that we can find all we need to know about our faith in the Bible, Latter Day Saints have other sources of authority. The only Bible they accept is the King James Bible, and they qualify that by saying "as far as correctly translated."

Gospel Principles is a manual printed as a guide for teachers and special study by the LDS Church. It explains the belief in authority this way: "The Church of Jesus Christ of Latter-day Saints accepts four books as scripture: the Bible, the Book of Mormon, the *Doctrine and Covenants*, and the *Pearl of Great Price*. These books are called the standard works of the Church. The inspired words of our living prophets are also accepted as scripture."[3] *Gospel Principles* continues to explain that the words of the prophets "come to us through conferences, Church publications, and instructions to local priesthood leaders.[4]

Mormons also believe that the current president and prophet of the LDS Church has authority from God to speak about spiritual things and that church members are to receive them as authoritative, on a level with scripture. This authority is especially true of "Special Pronouncements of the first presidency." The LDS prophet/president and his two counselors make up the First Presidency of the church. When these leaders make a pronouncement, the faithful are to understand them as "pronouncements from the LDS church." In other words, they recognize them as part of God's special revelation. Two such pronouncements were made in recent years: "The Living Christ" from January 1, 2000, and "The Proclamation on Family" from September 23, 1995.

Mormons view their Church president as a prophet, a voice piece of God. Twice each year, once in April and once in

October, LDS people gather in Salt Lake City for a general church conference. The leaders of the church speak to the twenty thousand people gathered in the LDS conference center, and the LDS satellite network carries it worldwide. Local Wards do not meet on that Sunday as the people are encouraged to remain home and "watch conference." In Utah, the local NBC station, which is LDS owned, televises the complete conference. Around the world, the faithful gather at their ward buildings and watch on satellite. When the prophet speaks to the people in conference, he speaks with the authority of God.

These basic differences in Mormon and Evangelical thought concerning the source of Special Revelation contain the roots of many of the doctrinal differences we will look at in later chapters. It explains the two-guidebook problem we have in relating to one another. It is impossible to overstate the importance of understanding our differing views of revelation when dealing with Mormon friends.

When Evangelicals think of a prophet, we are thinking of somebody who spoke the word of God. When I think of an apostle, I think of the twelve apostles in the New Testament and of Paul as the thirteenth. Everything that any person I accept as an apostle wrote is scripture to me. It is recorded in the New Testament, and I read it and study it. In the LDS church structure, however, since the first presidency, they have named and installed twelve apostles. Naturally then, from my own background and understanding I expected the writings of their apostles to be scripture for them. In this thinking, as I learned from my studies, I am mistaken.

When I think of a prophet's sermon or his writing, I am thinking of the Old Testament prophets. Evangelicals hold sacred everything Isaiah spoke and everything he wrote. Even though he wrote centuries before Christ, we study the book, we examine the passages, and we look at it verse-by-verse, word-by-word. We try to discover the meaning of the original words. We try to put it into the historical context in which it was written. Even though it was so long ago, we believe that the prophet was speaking the word of God then and that it is still the word of God today.

Our natural tendency is to think that Mormons believe the same way about the teachings and writings of their prophets. We ascribe our way of thinking about prophets to their thinking about their prophets. In our understanding, they would feel the same way about Brigham Young's words, especially words in his sermons and writings while he was the prophet, that we feel about Ezekiel's or Isaiah's. Again, we are mistaken. Our LDS friends and neighbors believe that special revelation did not cease in the first century with the death of the first apostles. They believe special revelation continues today in the words and writings of the current prophet. They understand that revelation very differently, however, from the revelations of their original leaders.

Continuing Revelation

While Evangelicals and most other Christians believe that revelation ended with the New Testament, Mormons believe that it is ongoing. BYU Professor Robert Millet says, "Well I suppose you could say that the latter day saints believe the canon of scripture is open, flexible, and expanding!"[5] By open, he means there can be more of it, that Scripture has not all been written and is continuing to be written today. Flexible means that over time scripture can change. Just because something was scripture in 1875 doesn't make it scripture today. Expanding suggests that our Bibles should be loose leaf so new pages of scripture can be inserted and existing pages can be deleted as changes are made.

Current apostle Dallin Oaks says, "What makes us different from most other Christians in the way we read and use the Bible and other scriptures is our belief in continuing revelation. For us, the scriptures are not the ultimate source of knowledge, but what precedes the ultimate source. The ultimate knowledge comes by revelation."[6] By revelation, Apostle Oaks means continuing revelation.

Evangelicals can look at a doctrine of faith and then return to the past to look at what theologians thought about it. We study doctrine by studying the teachings of Spurgeon,

Calvin, and others. While there may be a touch of disagreement on minor issues, basically we believe the same theology that was taught five hundred years ago.

For Mormons those things are not important. Their belief in continuing revelation means that what Mormons of the past had to say is not very important since they can discover truth by seeking it from the current prophet. On a trip to the LDS church office building to visit with one of the twelve LDS apostles, I read a portion of a Mormon classic, *A Marvelous Work and A Wonder,* that was written by LeGrand Richards, an apostle of the recent past. The current apostle, Neal Maxwell, commented to me about this book, "I don't believe that."[7] I found that statement very interesting. Here is one apostle who does not believe what another apostle said. While that may not make sense to non-Mormons, it is consistent to a Mormon. They believe that revelation is open, flexible, and expanding. What was truth for one age may not be truth in another. Truth can change.

I do not think we can over stress this. In our conversations with our friends, this is a key understanding. For an evangelical, doctrine has not changed, and it will not change. We believe that the doctrine that Paul taught was the doctrine that true Christians have taught through the ages. Our LDS neighbors do not have that belief, and this misconception can cause us to begin telling them what they are supposed to believe. That is never received well.

Listening Rather Than Telling.

Many times, in our concern for our Mormon friends, we go to a conference or read a book written by a well-meaning believer who has studied Mormonism. There we learn what he has discovered by studying Mormon history, documents, and scripture. When we talk to our Mormon friends about these strange beliefs, many times we discover they have never heard of such a doctrine, and they definitely do not believe it. I will consider some of these doctrines in their proper chapter. This misunderstanding may cause Mormons to accuse us of trying to tell them what they believe. It is important to let our Mormon friends tell us what they believe.

UNDERSTANDING THE LDS VIEW OF THE BIBLE

In addition to their extra scripture, Mormons also have two observations about the Bible that we need to understand. They believe that the Bible has been mistranslated, and they believe there are other books that should be in the Bible. The idea of mistranslation is presented in the eighth Article of Faith of the LDS Church, which states, "The Bible is true only as far as it is correctly translated. Joseph Smith felt that many plain and precious truths had been taken from the Bible before the documents were compiled into what we now know as the old and new testaments."[8]

When I first started to pastor a church in Utah, I met with some LDS missionaries. I knew they would claim that the Bible was translated incorrectly. When one of them made that claim, I opened my Greek New Testament and said, "I don't understand what you mean. Show me where it is translated incorrectly." I handed him my Greek New Testament, and it was Greek to him. He did not know how to translate the passage or even if I had handed him the right passage. That, however, is not what he was talking about when he said mistranslation. What those missionaries meant, and what is the understanding of our LDS friends, is that the Bible we use has been transmitted incorrectly. They believe that the original authors of the New Testament wrote using Greek. Later someone in the church translated it into Latin. Later still, medieval churchmen translated it from the Latin into English with the King James Version. Somewhere in the process from Greek to Latin to English, the Bible was "mistranslated."

That is not what we understand translation to mean. The Bible translations that we use are translated from manuscripts dated earlier than the manuscripts used by the King James translators. The primary Bibles in use in the seventeenth century were in Latin. The King James, however, was not translated from Latin, but from earlier Greek and Hebrew manuscripts. Likewise, most modern translations are not translated from the King James Version or from Latin, but from the original Greek and Hebrew.

The King James Version, the New International Version, The New American Standard Bible, and the rest of the modern translations are translated from the original languages. Overwhelming evidence points to the accuracy of the original language texts that we have today. What our neighbor really believes is that the transmission of the text was corrupt. It has nothing to do with the translation of manuscripts.

The Mormon's second objection to the Bible is that it is incomplete. They believe the early church voted not to accept some books that should be a part of the Bible. They believe that this omission happened before the King James Version was translated, during the early church conferences when deceptive church authorities voted to keep some books out of the Bible. The Book of Mormon expresses this belief: "Wherefore, thou seest that after the book hath gone forth through the hands of the great and abominable church, that there are many plain and precious things taken away from the book, which is the book of the Lamb of God" (1 Nephi 13:28).

This understanding of the compilation of the Bible as a vote of members of the church comes naturally for the Latter Day Saint. That is the way they have added to their own canon of scripture. Professor Millet explains how some of the prophecies of early Mormon presidents became scripture: "But in 1976 they were added to the standard works, the canon, *by a vote of the Church,* thus making them canonized scripture and as such they become binding upon the saints."[9] He then stated, "By 1880 the entire Church *voted* to accept the *Pearl of Great Price* as the fourth standard work, the fourth book of scripture in the LDS canon."[10] The action of their own church in deciding the canon of scripture has colored their view of how the Bible came to us. It would never occur to them that nineteenth century Mormons could have mistakenly voted false scripture into the church. They are sure, though, that an abominable and corrupt early church simply chose to vote out books that belong in the Bible. In these books are some of the precious truths that have

11

been lost. In our discussions with them, they might point to other books mentioned in the Old Testament, like "the book of the wars of the kings," and the Mormon will ask, "Why aren't these in the Bible?" Then they will answer their own question by saying the early church voted which books were to be in the canon and which ones were not. That is their understanding of how the canon came to be. With the restoration of the true church through Joseph Smith, special revelation was reopened, and the canon of scripture is never complete.

EVANGELICAL UNDERSTANDING OF THE BIBLE

An understanding on our part of the formation of the canon of scripture will help us in our discussions. It probably will not make any difference in their perception, but it will help us to understand truth and to understand their thinking.

The earliest church had no need for written documents. Their teachers were the apostles, the ones who had been with Jesus. Their Bible was the Old Testament interpreted in the light of the resurrection. The New Testament came about because of the respect the early church had for the apostles. Churches began to keep the words that they received from their leaders. As the church grew, it became impossible for the twelve to handle all the questions. As the number of Gentile converts grew, many who came into the church had never seen an apostle. Therefore, the church began to collect and preserve the writings of the apostles.

When heresy became a problem in the early church, the church leaders decided they needed to finalize the canon. The canon is the list of books that became the Bible. The Old Testament was already set, so they just needed to decide on what should comprise the New Testament. The process they used was more a formula than a vote. Their formula consisted of four criteria. 1) The document must have been written by an eyewitness or the scribe of an eyewitness. They wanted scripture that came from one of the original twelve apostles or one with apostolic authority. 2) The authorship of the document must be known and corroborated. 3) The document had to be in use in the churches. 4) It must be accepted as authoritative by the churches. Using this process over a period of years, the church finally settled on the books they considered authoritative.

Inspiration: What Does It Mean?

One of the areas in which we read from a different guidebook than our Mormon friends is on the concept of the inspiration of scripture. Bruce McConkie, who was one of the twelve Mormon apostles, published a book on Mormon doctrine that is still available at Deseret Book today. It is an LDS standard that the church has recently updated and republished. He says, "Only a few fanatics among the sects of Christendom profess to believe in what they call a 'verbal revelation,' that is, every word and syllable in some version of the Bible or another is the exact word spoken by Deity."[11]

Many of us Evangelicals are what McConkie calls fanatics. We believe in the Plenary Verbal doctrine of inspiration. That means two things. "Verbal" means that the very words of the Bible are inspired. God did not just inspire the thoughts; he inspired the very words. If we did not believe in verbal inspiration, there would be no point to a word study. We would never look at a Greek word and ask, "Why did Paul choose this word over another word? Why did Jesus use this word for church, instead of another word he could have used for church?" In the Sermon on the Mount Jesus says, "Think not that I am come to destroy the law, or the prophets: I am not come to destroy, but to fulfil. For verily I say unto you, Till heaven and earth pass, one jot or one tittle shall in no wise pass from the law, till all be fulfilled" (Matthew 5:17-18). Jesus said that even the small strokes are inspired. We believe the very words of scripture are inspired.

Plenary is a word that means complete. That means that every single part of the Bible is inspired. Leviticus is as inspired as the Gospel of John is inspired. Some Christians believe that just the Gospels are inspired. Others believe that the New Testament is all that is inspired. Most evangelicals, however, believe the Bible is inspired in all its parts, even to the choosing of one word over another. God allowed men to use their own styles. The letters of Paul do not sound like the letters of Peter, or of John. They each used their own style in writing, but the Holy Spirit inspired them to the choosing of one word over another.

I am one of the fanatics about whom McConkie was talking. I believe every word and every syllable in the original manuscripts are God's word to us. Since Mormons do not believe that, we have those different guidebooks concerning revelation.

The Bible is unique in that it is the best-attested document in terms of reliability. There is great evidence that the Bible we hold in our hands today has been reliably and accurately transmitted over the years. There are more than 5,300 known Greek manuscripts of the New Testament alone. Added to that are over 10,000 copies of Latin translations such as the Vulgate and another 9,300 other early versions. More than 24,000 manuscript copies of various portions of the New Testament are in existence today. It has been said that no other document of antiquity even begins to approach such numbers and attestation. As a comparison, the second best attested document is the Iliad by Homer, for which only 643 manuscripts are in existence.

In attesting the reliability of the Old Testament, one of the greatest modern discoveries for confirming the truthfulness and accuracy of the Old Testament was made in February or March of 1947. A Bedouin shepherd boy named Muhammad who was searching for a lost goat tossed a stone through a hole in a cliff on the west side of the Dead Sea. This cave is about eight miles south of Jericho. Instead of hearing the bleating of his goats, he heard the sound of shattering pottery. On investigating this surprising sound, he discovered several large jars containing leather scrolls wrapped in linen cloth. Someone had carefully sealed the jars, preserving the scrolls in excellent condition for nearly 1900 years. Some of these scrolls comprised ancient manuscripts of the Old Testament, predating the earliest known manuscripts by 900 years. One scroll was the entire text of the book of Isaiah. These Dead Sea Scrolls proved beyond any doubt that the Hebrew text we have is accurate. Gleason Archer, a

Harvard Ph.D., says this concerning the Dead Sea Manuscripts of the Old Testament prophet Isaiah: "They proved to be word for word identical with our standard Hebrew Bible in more than 95% of the text. The 5% of variation consisted chiefly of obvious slips of the pen and variations in spelling."[12] Where there were variations, none of them changed the meaning of the text in any significant way. The truth is, the text of both the Old Testament and the New has been transmitted accurately, so much so that we can say this book we hold in our hands is a miraculous book, inspired of God.

Inspiration and Illumination

When we are dealing with theology, our words need to be precise. Paul tells the young pastor Timothy, "All scripture *is* given by inspiration of God, and *is* profitable for doctrine, for reproof, for correction, for instruction in righteousness: That the man of God may be perfect, thoroughly furnished unto all good works " (2 Timothy 3:16-17).

Evangelicals and Mormons differ concerning what we believe about inspiration. Evangelicals believe that inspiration takes place in three categories. The first category is Manifestations. A manifestation is an act of God where He breaks into history for a particular redemptive purpose. He does not do that often, but He does do it. He breaks into our time and makes Himself known in one way or another. His greatest manifestation was in the birth, ministry, death, and resurrection of Jesus Christ.

The second classification is Inspiration. Inspire means to breathe. What Paul is saying in 2 Timothy is that all scripture is breathed by God. "Knowing this first, that no prophecy of the scripture is of any private interpretation. For the prophecy came not in old time by the will of man: but holy men of God spake *as they were* moved by the Holy Ghost" (2 Peter 1:20-21).

We call the third category of what God is doing Illumination. Illumination is the act of God enabling men in every age to understand and appropriate the meaning of His redemptive acts and of things sufficient for salvation and

15

effective Christian living. Here is the difference between inspiration and illumination. When we hear a sermon on Sunday morning, we may leave saying, "That was inspired by God." Precisely, however, the only thing inspired by God is the reading of scripture. The scripture is fundamentally different from anything the preacher can do. Our technical understanding of inspiration is that if God inspired anything the preacher said, it is God breathed, and we should transcribe it off the tape, print it, and add it to the end of our Bible.

Scripture is that which God inspired. Illumination is what the Spirit does in my life that allows me to understand and interpret what has been inspired already. In our normal speech and process we don't make a differentiation between inspiration and illumination. God inspired the writers of scripture. God illumines us. He allows the light of his grace to shine in our hearts, in our minds, and in our understanding so that all of a sudden we understand Him better than ever before. However, that was for us, and maybe for somebody with whom we can share it, but it was not for the church as a whole.

As we study the beliefs of our LDS friends and neighbors, we need to remember the two guidebooks. If our discussion is to be significant, we must understand not only our own guidebook, but theirs as well.

2

The Book of Mormon

Another Testament of Jesus Christ

For the Latter-day Saint, the Book of Mormon is more than just an additional book of scripture. Most Mormons esteem the Book of Mormon above the other works of scripture. Mormons state that it is "the most truthful of all the books on the face of the earth." They believe the Book of Mormon to be the scriptural foundation of their church. It is another book of scripture on a level of, and even above, the Bible, since they believe the Bible is incorrectly translated.

The subtitle of the book is "Another testament of Jesus Christ." For the Latter-day Saint the Book of Mormon is a further testimony of Jesus Christ. "Mormons believe the Old Testament is the record of the prophets of God who lived on the earth before Jesus was born, but who taught Christianity and the basic principles of the Gospel of Jesus Christ."[13] According to them, The Law of Moses as given in the Old Testament is a stricter version of the Gospel because the people were unwilling to live the Christ-like version of the Gospel. The New Testament is the record of Jesus' time on earth with his disciples, and the Book of Mormon is another testimony of the gospel of Christ given to the inhabitants of the Americas. Thus there are three testimonies, or testaments, of Jesus Christ.

The Book of Mormon describes Jesus' appearance on the American continent after His ascension in Acts 1, an appearance prophesied by Jesus himself in his words to the disciples. In John 10:14-16 Jesus talks about other sheep that belong to him, and Mormons believe that the peoples inhabiting the Americas were those other sheep.

THE STORY OF THE BOOK OF MORMON

A young Joseph Smith claimed that an angel visited him several times. At first the angel revealed some gold plates buried in the earth along with a breast plate and two stones, a Umim and a Thumim, that were to be used for translating the plates. Joseph was only allowed to look at the treasure in the earth; he was not allowed to take it. The angel showed the plates to young Joseph every year for four years. After that time the angel allowed him to get the plates and translate them. Joseph claimed the angel told Joseph his name was Moroni and that his father Mormon had made the plates. Joseph set about translating the plates using the two stones. While he was translating, he received further visits from heavenly personages and received, along with the Book of Mormon, a restored Gospel.

THE STORY IN THE BOOK OF MORMON

The Book of Mormon is the story of two migrations from the Middle East to the Americas. The first occurred after the destruction of the tower of Babel. This group of travelers was the Jaredites. The second and more important of the migrations took place around 600 BC, before the fall of Jerusalem. The Book of Mormon is an abridged account of their records by a prophet/historian named Mormon. The people who came to the Americas in 600 BC separated into two nations, known as the Nephites and the Lamanites.

The book of 3 Nephi contains the account of the ministry of Jesus Christ to the Nephites in America. In this book, Jesus appears to them and teaches the message from the Sermon on the Mount. Jesus prays for the Nephites and tells them He has still other sheep. Jesus sets up a church with another set of twelve disciples and gives them the authority to baptize. He teaches them the sacraments. In chapter 18 He ascends into heaven In the next chapter He reappears and continues to teach and minister. In chapter 28 Mormon takes over, and Jesus disappears from the Narrative.

The story of the Book of Mormon culminates in a final battle in which the Lamanites exterminate the Nephites. The prophet-leader Mormon compiles the record on metal plates with the help of his son, Moroni. They bury the plates in what later becomes New York State. In 1823, Moroni returns as an angel to present the plates to Joseph Smith. Joseph translates them and presents them to the world.

Concerning the Book of Mormon Joseph Smith writes, "I told the brethren that the Book of Mormon was the most correct of any book on earth, the keystone of our religion and a man could get nearer to God by abiding in its precepts than by any other book."[14] Latter-day Saints principally believe this about the Book of Mormon. They believe that if people will read it and pray about it, God will show them that it is true. For that reason, they actively try to get the book into the hands of as many people as they possibly can.

The Book of Mormon in the Bible

Mormons interpret certain biblical passages to show the Book of Mormon in the Bible. The first and most often used is Ezekiel 37:16-17.

> Moreover, thou son of man, take thee one stick, and write upon it, For Judah, and for the children of Israel his companions: then take another stick, and write upon it, For Joseph, the stick of Ephraim, and *for* all the house of Israel his companions: And join them one to another into one stick; and they shall become one in thine hand.

The Mormon interpretation of this prophecy is that the sticks described here are scrolls. There is the scroll written for Judah and the scroll written for Joseph. The Bible is the stick of Judah; the Book of Mormon is the Stick of Ephraim, who was one of Joseph's sons. Then, with Moroni's revelation of the Book of Mormon in 1830, they were joined together. The Mormon understanding is that the Ezekiel prophecy proves the authenticity of the Book of Mormon and its legitimacy as a companion of the Bible.

A second prophecy with a Book of Mormon interpretation is found in Isaiah.

> And the vision of all is become unto you as the words of a book that is sealed, which *men*

deliver to one that is learned, saying, Read this, I pray thee: and he saith, I cannot; for it *is* sealed: And the book is delivered to him that is not learned, saying, Read this, I pray thee: and he saith, I am not learned. "Wherefore the Lord said, Forasmuch as this people draw near *me* with their mouth, and with their lips do honour me, but have removed their heart far from me, and their fear toward me is taught by the precept of men: Therefore, behold, I will proceed to do a marvellous work among this people, *even* a marvellous work and a wonder: for the wisdom of their wise *men* shall perish, and the understanding of their prudent *men* shall be hid" (Isaiah 29:11-14).

In Mormon understanding, the sealed book is the Book of Mormon, and when it is opened, as it was in 1830, a marvelous work results.

One New Testament passage relating to the events of the Book of Mormon is the other sheep passage from the Gospel of John: "And other sheep I have, which are not of this fold: them also I must bring, and they shall hear my voice; and there shall be one fold, *and* one shepherd" (John 10:16). LDS belief states that the other sheep described here are the descendants of the Hebrews who had left Jerusalem six hundred years earlier and were now living in the Americas.

Mormon teaching and proselytizing use these three passages extensively. They are sure that they point to the Book of Mormon, its discovery and publication, and the events that it details. (In LDS circles proselytizing is used in a positive sense, much as we use the word evangelizing.)

An Evangelical Response to the Claims of the Book of Mormon

It is important to be able to explain the Book of Mormon phenomena and accurately handle the scriptures. Arguments will not persuade a convinced Mormon. They believe the Book of Mormon is true because it is their testimony that upon praying about its truthfulness, they received confirmation from God that it is true. They hear this testimony countless times every Sunday at their ward meetings. It is repeated over and over again. If they grew up LDS, they began hearing it as babies. It is drilled into them.

Prophecies in the Bible

How do we respond to the claims of our LDS friends that the Bible has prophecies regarding the Book of Mormon?

The first principle of biblical interpretation is to read passages in their context. For example, in reading the verses around the verses used to support their claim and putting them in their proper context, Ezekiel's meaning becomes clear. It is not a prophecy regarding books or scrolls. Verse 22 explains the meaning of the sticks.

> And the sticks whereon thou writest shall be in thine hand before their eyes. And say unto them, Thus saith the Lord GOD; Behold, I will take the children of Israel from among the heathen, whither they be gone, and will gather them on every side, and bring them into their own land: And I will make them one nation in the land upon the mountains of Israel; and one king shall be king to them all: and they shall be no more two nations, neither shall they be divided into two kingdoms any more at all: Neither shall they defile themselves any more with their idols, nor with their detestable things, nor with any of their transgressions: but I will save them out of all their dwellingplaces, wherein they have sinned, and will cleanse them: so shall they be my people, and I will be their God (Ezekiel 37:20-23).

After the death of Solomon, his sons and his servants split Israel into two nations. Israel was the name of the nation containing the ten northern tribes, and the nation of Judah consisted of the two southern tribes, Judah and Benjamin. Judah was the largest and most prominent of the two tribes, giving the nation its name.

Israel is the usual name for the northern tribes, but the Bible sometimes uses Joseph or Ephraim because Ephraim was the largest tribe in the north. Serious Bible scholars know that Ezekiel 37 is a prophecy that God is going to reunite the kingdoms one day. The sticks are representations of the tribal nations of the Hebrews, not of books.

The Mormon interpretation of the prophecy of Isaiah 29 is a fanciful interpretation to which they turn because of the Book of Mormon reference. A more likely interpretation is that the sealed book in Isaiah is the one the Lamb of God opens in Revelation 5. In any extent, there is no reason, outside of LDS claims, to assume their interpretation is correct.

In their interpretation of the John 10 passage, Mormons are making suppositions about the identification of the other sheep. The simplest and most direct meaning of the passage is that Jesus is talking about the Gentiles. He is asserting that He did not come just for the Jews. He came also for the Gentiles. The other sheep He is talking about are you and me. We are the Gentiles grafted in, and we belong to the Lord. The understanding that God considers the Gentiles his sheep explains the anger of the Jews in verse 19. Why would the Jews have gotten angry enough to kill Jesus if He was talking about people they knew nothing of in a land about which they had never heard? They were angry because Jesus was accepting the hated Gentiles.

Another Testament of Jesus Christ

The Book of Mormon subtitle, *Another Testament of Jesus Christ*, presents a view of the testaments different from that of Christianity. Using testament as a synonym for testimony, they believe the Book of Mormon is another testimony concerning Jesus Christ and the Gospel. Other than being a little stricter in the Old Testament, it is the same gospel.

In Christian understanding, the word testament does not mean testimony. Testament is a word that comes from the word for covenant. We believe that the Bible is a record of God's covenants with humankind. The Old Covenant is the covenant of law, including the Ten Commandments, that God made through Moses. With the advent of Jesus Christ, his death, his burial, and his resurrection, God made a new covenant with humankind through the church. This is the covenant of grace. The Old Testament records the Old Covenant; the New Testament records the New Covenant. In Mormon thinking, however, the Book of Mormon is not another covenant between God and humankind. In their understanding, all three works, the Old Testament, The New Testament, and the Book of Mormon are three testimonies of the only covenant with God.

The Book of Mormon Challenge

When proselytizing, Mormons often present this challenge: "Have you read the Book of Mormon and prayed about it?" They believe that if a prospect will read it and pray about it, God will reveal the truth of the Book of Mormon. After all, that is how God revealed the truth to Joseph Smith. Like Smith, they quote the New Testament letter of James: "If any of you lack wisdom, let him ask of God, that giveth to all *men* liberally, and upbraideth not; and it shall be given him" (James 1:5).

There is a parallel passage in the Book of Mormon: "And when ye shall receive these things, I would exhort you that ye would ask God, the Eternal Father, in the name of Christ, if these things are not true; and if ye shall ask with a sincere heart, with real intent, having faith in Christ, he will manifest the truth of it unto you, by the power of the Holy Ghost" (Moroni 10:4).

It is neither necessary nor Biblical to read the Book of Mormon and then to pray about it to come to a decision about its veracity. We do not need to pray about everything before we know God's truth. It is not necessary, for example, for me to pray about whether or not I should commit adultery. I know that it would not be okay to rob a bank because we need money. Scripture is clear about sexual purity and honesty.

The Bible also tells us how to discover the truth. For example, Paul's encouragement is to "prove all things; hold fast that which is good" (1 Thessalonians 5:21). The Bible does not recommend praying about it to see if it is right. The Bible's

23

solution is to examine things. I have had people, Baptists, not Mormons, say to me, "I have been praying about it, and it is okay for me to have an affair." How do I respond to this? I tell them God does not speak that way. I tell them they must examine God's word. What does God say? True believers read his word and hold fast to that which is good.

In the book of Acts, Luke praised the Berean believers for their biblical examination. "These were more noble than those in Thessalonica, in that they received the word with all readiness of mind, and searched the scriptures daily, whether those things were so. Therefore many of them believed; also of honourable women which were Greeks, and of men, not a few" (Acts 17:11-12).

John's exhortation was to test the spirits. "Beloved, believe not every spirit, but try the spirits whether they are of God: because many false prophets are gone out into the world" (1 John 4:1).

Reading more of the passage in James makes it easier to understand his message.

> James, a servant of God and of the Lord Jesus Christ, to the twelve tribes which are scattered abroad, greeting. My brethren, count it all joy when ye fall into divers temptations; Knowing *this*, that the trying of your faith worketh patience. But let patience have *her* perfect work, that ye may be perfect and entire, wanting nothing. If any of you lack wisdom, let him ask of God, that giveth to all *men* liberally, and upbraideth not; and it shall be given him (James 1:1-5).

James's encouragement here was to pray about trials and temptations. When we are tempted, James says, pray. We are to ask God to help us deal with the temptation. He was not talking about just throwing everything out, praying, and asking God to make us smart. Imagine prayer taking the place of thorough study and examination. That could really change things. Instead of going to school and getting an education, we could just pray and ask God to give us wisdom.

24

Examining The Book of Mormon

What does a careful examination of the Book of Mormon reveal? A comparison of the Book of Mormon and the Bible indicates a significant difference between the two. The Book of Mormon is a very different book than the Old and New Testaments. We will examine just a few of the ways in which it differs.

Linguistically the Book of Mormon is inadequate. A study of the language issues will convince an unbiased reader that something is wrong. The language claims fail in many ways.

According to Joseph Smith, the language on the golden plates from which he translated the Book of Mormon was Reformed Egyptian. History has discovered no such language as Reformed Egyptian. No one has ever seen any example of Reformed Egyptian. There is no evidence for it. With a unified voice modern Egyptologists deny that such a language ever existed. In the Book of Mormon we have a book translated from metal plates that are not now available, in a language that never existed, by a young man with no language training. These facts cause us to seriously doubt its legitimacy. The Mormons exalt that God could perform such a miracle. They actually stress Joseph Smith's lack of education as proof only God could do such a thing.

The Book of Mormon quotes the King James Version of the Bible quite liberally. Supposedly, Moroni and Mormon put the golden plates in the ground about AD 400; however, the translators authorized by King James to translate the Greek and Hebrew texts into English did not finish their work until 1611. This raises an interesting question. How does an earlier text quote a text written twelve hundred years later?

In the four hundred years since the 1611 edition of the King James Version, it has gone through many transformations. Because of natural growth in the English language, an edition of the original 1611 King James Version would be almost as difficult for us to read as an unknown language would. The King James Version quoted in the Book of Mormon is the edition that was widely available in 1830. The implication, of course, is that

Joseph Smith copied much of the Book of Mormon directly from the King James Bible. The translation did not come from golden plates. This circumstantial evidence points to plagiarism from the Bible rather than a transcription from a golden plate.

Mormons explain that when God gave the translation to Joseph Smith, God put it in the King James language. One interesting finding concerns the italicized words in the King James. If we read a standard translation of the Bible, one that tries to translate word for word as nearly as possible, we find that some words are italicized. When we find an italicized word, it is indication from the translators that a word has no corresponding word in the original language. They have added the English word in order for the translation to make sense. The translators want us to know that they added a word. They do this by italicizing it. When The Book of Mormon quotes the King James Version, even the italicized words are included. It is as if someone just copied a King James Bible.

The Book of Mormon passage found in Jacob 7:27 includes a French word, adieu. A discerning reader might wonder how a French word made its way into a Hebrew text written in reformed Egyptian hieroglyphics when the French language was not developed until AD 700?

The Grammar of the Book of Mormon falls short of its purportedly divine origin. The Mormon Church has changed the text of the Book of Mormon many times to correct the grammar. If the Book of Mormon was a divine translation, as claimed by the LDS church, the grammar should have been correct.

In the sciences of anthropology and ethnology there are problems with Smith's claims. Scientists have not authenticated any migration to America from the Semitic Peoples of the Middle East. Semitic people are those Jews and Arabs of the Middle East who are descendants of Abraham. If such a great migration occurred and grew into the great civilizations as described in the Book of Mormon, we would expect to find descendants of those people occupying the land. In fact, when Joseph first produced the Book of Mormon, that was his claim. The Native population of the Americas, however, did not descend from a Hebrew (Semite), but are Mongoloid in origin. Anthropologists have traced their migration to the Americas across the Bering Strait, then down the coast, and spreading across the continent.

As the scientific community came to understand the origins of the peoples in the Americas, Bruce R. McConkie, a late LDS apostle, added the following phrase to the introduction of the Book of Mormon in 1981. "After thousands of years, all were destroyed except the Lamanites, and they are the principal ancestors of the American Indians." This explanation was necessary to explain the non-Semitic nature of the American Indian.

DNA technology has proved a further difficulty for Latter-day Saints. It has made it necessary for the LDS Church to change the introduction to the Book of Mormon once again. In November 2007 they changed it to read, "After thousands of years, all were destroyed except the Lamanites, and they are among the ancestors of the American Indians." As our understanding of anthropology increases, the Lamanites have fallen from being the ancestors of American Indians, to being the principal ancestors of American Indians, to simply being among the ancestors of the American Indians.

Another problem Mormons face with their book is the lack of a Book of Mormon geography. There are continual attempts by LDS scholars to make a case that Central and South America are the sites of the events contained in the Book of Mormon. Joseph Smith thought that it was in New York and the Northeast. To date, archaeologists have not confirmed one single site mentioned in the Book of Mormon.

At Deseret Books and in Salt Lake City, even at Sam's Club, one can purchase large coffee table books of Mormon sites in the Americas. All of them are of Mayan or Incan sites, none of which archaeologists accept as the legitimate sites of events from the Book of Mormon.

Contrary to Mormon teaching, there is no new world Mormon Archeology. Attempts at a Book of Mormon archeology usually include the civilizations of the Aztecs, the Incas, and the Mayans. They attempt to make their ruins into some of the cities in the Book of Mormon. There are those who profess it. W. F.

27

Walker Johanson explains this archaeology in his Mormon apologetic book, *What is Mormonism all about*. He makes this argument.

> There are many archeologists who have made (and are continuing to make) efforts to find the locations in Central and South America that are described in the Book of Mormon, to see if indeed some of those places actually existed. There are many books that have been written that claim that such evidence has been found, and others that claim that the possible link to Book of Mormon claims is unsubstantiated.[15]

Johanson would agree that nobody can substantiate these claims.

On the grounds of the LDS Temple in Salt Lake City there are two visitor's centers. Downstairs in the North Visitors Center the LDS church has built a display that shows a Nephite prophet writing on a scroll. On the wall behind him is a collection of other scrolls. It is an interesting montage, but archeological evidence for any such manuscripts existing in the New World is lacking. No evidence has ever been found showing one single manuscript of any portion of the Book of Mormon, on scrolls or on metal plates. When a person compares the lack of manuscript evidence for the Book of Mormon to the fifty thousand manuscripts and fragments of the New Testament, it becomes clear where the archeology of the Book of Mormon is deficient.

There are other archeological inconsistencies. In the Book of Mormon steel is mentioned, but steel was not yet invented in AD 400. The Book of Mormon talks of wheeled wagons and other artifacts of a developed civilization not present in the New World. The Book of Mormon peoples had horses, but archeologists tell us that the introduction of horses to the New World came with the Spanish after Columbus.

To understand our Mormon friends we need to understand how they deal with these issues. Were an Evangelical to raise these objections, they would receive an answer similar to one I received when I brought this up with a returned missionary with whom I played golf one afternoon. His reply was, "You can't demand a sign. Some things you just have to take by faith."

W. F. Walker Johanson explains this thinking. He says, "You have to take some things by faith. Jesus pointed out people who are always looking for a sign. Jesus says that those who look for such signs have no faith, and are not believers."[16]

> Throughout history, people have looked for hard evidence – a splinter from the Cross at Calvary; a piece of leather from one of the Apostle Paul's sandals; the Ark of the Covenant; the Holy Grail; the Shroud of Turin. These are the same kinds of evidence that both believers and detractors have sought for centuries. God will withhold this evidence, it is not needed by Mormons in order for them to believe.[17]

This argument totally misses the point. We do not want hard evidence; we are not insisting that we have Nephi's crown, or robe, or anything in particular. We just want evidence that we are basing our faith on something true.

In the North Visitor's Center there is a display showing the city of Jerusalem as it is believed to have existed in Jesus' day. It is a beautiful and interesting display. It marks the places in Jerusalem where Biblical events took place. Scholars cannot pinpoint some of the exact places, but we do know the location of many others. The early Roman Church built the Church of the Holy Sepulcher over the place of the execution and burial of Jesus. The location of Herod's temple, the temple Jesus and the disciples visited in the Gospels, is known. One of the walls of the foundation of the temple platform remains until today and is a holy place for Jews.

When I was in seminary, I took a class in New Testament Archeology. The professor gave us a list of places in the New Testament. Our assignment was to pick out a place and give a report on it. We wrote the report for our class and presented it orally. On the day we gave our report, the professor used his slide projector and showed slides of the place we were studying that day. Each slide was from his journeys in the Holy Land.

For every single city in the New Testament, we can walk there, stand there, and say, "Today I stood where Jesus stood." In some cities it is possible to stand where Paul preached or Peter conversed with Jesus. Secular history records the emperors, governors, and officials of the New Testament. To a lesser extent the Old Testament is the same way. Some of the Old Testament is so far removed from today that it has not yet been verified.

Modern archeologists find a total lack of archeological evidence for the Book of Mormon. For example, there is the absence of coins discovered in the New World. In his gospel, Mark tells us about an incident in the life of Jesus.

> 41 And Jesus sat over against the treasury, and beheld how the people cast money into the treasury: and many that were rich cast in much. 42 And there came a certain poor widow, and she threw in two mites, which make a farthing. 43 And he called *unto him* his disciples, and saith unto them, Verily I say unto you. That this poor widow hath cast more in. than all they which have cast into the treasury: 44 For all *they* did cast in of their abundance: but she of her want did cast in all that she had even all her living (Mark 12:41-44).

This simple story of stewardship mentions the mite, a coin. I have in my possession a genuine mite from the first century. It is called a widow's mite. How could a poor Baptist preacher in Southern Utah ever get his hands on a widow's mite? This is a coin from two thousand years ago. I received it as a gift. The only reason I can own one is because of the abundance of this coin.

Anyone who has ever experimented with a metal detector knows the abundance of coins dropped in the dirt. We always hope that the beep indicating metal is pointing to a diamond ring hiding in the dirt. Alas, normally it is a penny. Sometimes we might find a dime or maybe a quarter. It is a fact. People drop coins.

If we are to believe the archeological record, we have to come to the conclusion that either there was never a Nephite civilization or that they were somehow so completely different from any other civilization that none of the Nephites ever dropped a coin. The Book of Mormon mentions coins, but there is no display of Nephite coins in any museum of the Americas. Coins of other civilizations are abundant wherever they were used, even in ancient Rome and Palestine. None, however, have been found in the New World.

Conclusion

Our LDS friends will not accept these arguments. I write them here for the benefit of our understanding. Their parents and Sunday school teachers from preschool have taught them that the Book of Mormon is true and is the basis for all belief. Where it disagrees with the Bible, they will choose the Book of Mormon because they have a current prophet of God to interpret right and wrong for them. The president, prophet, and seer of the Church is a good man and would never lead them astray.

They regularly repeat, and hear others repeat, their testimony of the Book of Mormon in the ward meetings. "I know the Book of Mormon is true." They have heard it repeated by the leaders in their city, county, and state. They know, despite all objections, that the Book of Mormon is true.

3
Other LDS Scripture

Joseph Smith as a Prophet and Translator

When our LDS neighbors pick up their scriptures and head to their ward building for sacrament meeting and Sunday School, they are picking up more than the Bible and the Book of Mormon. They have two other volumes of scripture. The *Doctrine and Covenants* is a collection of revelations given to Joseph Smith and a few other Mormon prophets and bound together in one book. The *Pearl of Great Price* contains other writings of Joseph Smith.

Doctrine and Covenants

The introduction of the *Doctrine and Covenants* gives this information.

> The Doctrine and Covenants is a collection of divine revelations and inspired declarations given for the establishment and regulation of the kingdom of God on the earth in the last days. Although most of the sections are directed to members of the Church of Jesus Christ of Latter-day saints, the messages, warnings, and exhortations are for the benefit of all mankind, and contain an invitation to all people everywhere to hear the voice of the Lord Jesus Christ, speaking to them for their temporal well-being and their everlasting salvation.[18]

The *Doctrine and Covenants* contains 138 sections. Each one is accepted as a direct revelation of God to the church, communicated through the prophet. At the end of the sections there are two "official declarations." Official Declaration 1 is from Wilford Woodruff, given in 1890, and forbids the practice of polygamy. Official Declaration 2 is the announcement that President Spencer Kimball received a revelation extending the priesthood and temple blessing to all worthy male members of the church. This 1978 revelation served to admit to the priesthood men from every race.

Most of the revelations were given to Joseph Smith during the early days of the church. Some are directions to guide the church; others are addressed to specific individuals and concern their personal matters. Section 135 is a description of the death of Joseph Smith written by Elder John Taylor. Section 136 is from Brigham Young concerning the makeup of the parties as they made their way west from Illinois to Utah. Section 138 is a revelation to Joseph Fielding Smith in 1918 and is a doctrinal matter concerning Jesus Christ and his time in the grave.

Some Teachings Found in the Doctrine and Covenants

Because they do not purport to be ancient scripture but revelations given to a living prophet, the teachings found in the *Doctrine and Covenants* have a contemporary ring. For example, Section 1:30 explains that the LDS church is the only true and living church.

After translating the first 116 pages of the Book of Mormon, Joseph Smith allowed Martin Harris to take the completed pages home to help convince Harris' wife of its truthfulness. She refused to return the pages, challenging Martin that if indeed it was a translation, Joseph should be able to retranslate them. Joseph Smith did not retranslate them. Sections 3 and 10 explain how the loss was foreknown by Mormon when he transcribed the plates and say that is the reason there was a condensation of the "Book of Lehi" already in the Golden Plates.

Section 20 concerns the organization of the church and includes the exact words that must be recited whenever there is a baptism and each Sunday when the sacrament is blessed. Section 57 identifies Independence, Missouri, as the place for the City of Zion and the first LDS temple. Section 84 asserts that the New Jerusalem would be built in Missouri. Section 89 contains the Word of Wisdom. The Word of Wisdom is the teaching concerning the command to abstain from wine, strong drinks, tobacco, and hot drinks, which today pretty much means coffee.

The Mormon handbook, *Gospel Principles*, describes the *Doctrine and Covenants* this way. "This book contains the revelations regarding the Church of Jesus Christ as it has been restored in these last days. Several sections of the book explain the organization of the Church and define the offices of the priesthood and their function."[19]

Gospel Principles describes some of the sections. "For example sections 76 and 88 contain glorious truths lost to the world for hundreds of years."[20] Basically these "glorious truths" are references to three separate heavens and concern the people who inhabit other worlds. Sections 29 and 93 shed light on teachings in the Bible. Section 133 contains prophecy of events to come.

Section 132 is about polygamy. It is called the new and everlasting covenant. The revelation was given in 1843, but according to the preface of the section Joseph Smith had known about it since 1831.

Our LDS friends and neighbors believe this collection of revelations is sacred scripture. It holds the authority of the Bible and the Book of Mormon. Over the years there were additions and subtractions, leading to the current edition, which was published in 1981.

The Pearl of Great Price

The other book among the LDS standard works is *The Pearl of Great Price*. It is the inspired writings of the Prophet Joseph Smith. It contains five sections, including the books of Moses and Abraham. The Book of Moses contains visions and writings of Moses that were revealed to Joseph Smith. They are an extract from the book of Genesis in Joseph Smith's translation of the Bible.

According to Mormon tradition, Joseph Smith translated The Book of Abraham from a papyrus scroll he purchased from a traveling salesman in 1835. His claim was that the scroll contained writings of the patriarch Abraham. There is a reinterpretation of Matthew 23:39 and Matthew 24 as it is found in the Joseph Smith Translation of the Bible. There are some other writings from Joseph Smith, including some of his testimony and some of the history of the church he wrote in 1838.

The last section is The Articles of Faith of The Church of Jesus Christ of Latter-day Saints.

Book of Abraham

The Book of Abraham is unique among Mormon scripture. It is the one piece of Joseph Smith's translations for which there is a manuscript in existence. This manuscript allows for the evaluation of Smith's ability as a translator.

Apostle Bruce McConkie says of this book,

> This work was translated by the Prophet from a papyrus record taken from the catacombs of Egypt, a record preserved by the Lord to come forth in this day of restoration. Abraham was the original author, and the scriptural account contains priceless information about the gospel, pre-existence, the nature of Deity, the creation, and priesthood, information which is not otherwise available in any other revelation now extant.[21]

In July 1835 Joseph Smith met Michael H. Chandler in Kirtland, Ohio. Chandler was a traveling showman who was displaying four Egyptian mummies. Along with the mummies, Chandler possessed two rolls of papyri that contained a number of hieroglyphics. He sold these papyri to the Mormons for $2,400. The next day, Smith proclaimed that the biblical Abraham and Joseph had actually written these papyri. The introduction to the Book of Abraham makes the claim that this papyrus is written "by his [Abraham's] own hand."

The book of Abraham is five chapters dealing primarily with Abraham's visit to Egypt and the things the Lord showed him there by using the Urim and the Thummim. He learned new names for the sun, moon, and stars and learned of the existence of the planet Kolob. This planet is the one nearest to the throne of God.

Chapters 4 and 5 tell the creation story of Genesis 1 and 2 with a slight twist. Instead of being the work of God, it is the work of the gods. Included in the book of Abraham are three "facsimiles" that appear to have been taken from the papyri.

If this story of the papyri was all true, what a priceless find they would be. One could almost make an argument that the biblical Joseph might have known how to write something in Egyptian. After all, he grew up there, beginning as a slave and eventually becoming a high government official. It would be a little harder to understand why Abraham would have written a document in Egyptian although the Old Testament recounts his two visits to Egypt.

The major problem with accepting the book of Abraham as authentic is that when Joseph Smith came into possession of these papyri in 1835, the interpretation of Egyptian hieroglyphics was in its infancy. The Rosetta Stone that was discovered in 1799 by Napoleon's army in Egypt contained the code that eventually allowed Egyptologists to understand Egyptian hieroglyphics. This discovery was likely unknown in Ohio in 1835. Neither Joseph Smith, nor anyone else in Ohio, would have known that Egyptologists were close to breaking the code of hieroglyphics.

As far as is known, Joseph Smith never attempted to translate the papyri that he attributed to Joseph. At some point the papyri disappeared. For over one hundred years they were thought to have burned in the great Chicago fire. In 1967 the papyri were found again in the Metropolitan Museum of Art in New York City. Because of the advances in understanding Egyptian writing, Egyptologists could now translate them. These trained scholars unanimously declared the manuscripts to be ordinary funeral papyri dating from around the time of Christ. This decision caused two problems. As ancient as these papyri were, they were two thousand years too young for Abraham to be the author. The more pressing problem was that the Egyptologist's translation had no resemblance to Joseph Smith's translation.

The LDS church had to respond to this discovery. Officially the LDS Church does not deny the authenticity of the documents, but there have been several different responses. Some Mormon scholars claim the 1967 papyri are not the same as those Joseph Smith translated. The late Hugh Nibly, a respected and revered Mormon scholar and apologist, took this approach. However, research proves otherwise. Papyrus is a plant based paper and is very fragile. Much of the NT was written originally on papyrus, and not much remains but fragments. The Egyptian burial process and the dry Egyptian tombs in the desert combined to keep these funeral papyri in decent condition. Even so, when the purchasers opened them in 1835 they began to crack and break. Because they were very fragile, their Mormon owners tried to protect them by attaching a backing to hold them together. The papers that served as backing contained Mormon related things such as architectural drawings of a temple and maps of the Kirtland, Ohio, area. These backings are on the papyri discovered in 1967. All evidence points to these documents being the same one that Joseph Smith possessed.

A second Mormon response is that modern Egyptologists are inaccurate and Joseph Smith is the correct translator. A more creative response is that the papyri contain dual meanings. One meaning is the one the Egyptologists say is there; the other is the meaning that Joseph Smith gave to them. Perhaps the most creative answer is that as Joseph Smith meditated on the writings, certain images brought to mind the revelation that God was trying to give to him so that it is authentic. This is much the same manner Joseph Smith used in his retranslation of the Bible. While Evangelicals have real problems with this last answer, it does not cause a problem with our LDS friends because they start with the belief that Joseph Smith was a true prophet and seer and had a special gift of translation.

Our Mormon friend could believe any of these answers if he or she even thinks about it at all. There is no official LDS Church response to these questions.

Teachings from *The Pearl of Great Price*

It is in *The Pearl of Great Price* that Mormons learn of God's relationship to the planet Kolob. Kolob is the planet that is closest to the celestial kingdom, which is the residence of God. (See Appendix VII) The book of Abraham teaches that Adam himself was baptized in the name of Jesus Christ and was given the priesthood. The Book of Moses contains the teaching that Jesus volunteered to become the savior of the world and that his plan was the one God chose instead of the plan of Lucifer.

In Summary Regarding Revelation

Evangelicals believe that God's final revelation of Himself is in Jesus Christ (Hebrews 1:1-3). In the past, according to the perspective of the writer of Hebrews, God spoke through his prophets, but in these last days God has spoken to us by his Son. The Bible's view is that the era of direct revelation by prophecy has passed. The reason the book of Hebrews gives for the ending of the era of prophecy is that the one to whom the prophets pointed, Jesus Christ, has come. All the law and the prophets point to Jesus Christ, all the Old Testament is pointing to Jesus Christ, and now He has come. God is speaking in these last days in his Son.

How does He do that? God spoke to the first century world when Jesus Christ came into the world. God continues to speak to us concerning his Son through the New Testament. The gospels are the record of Jesus Christ. They tell us his story, how He lived, how He was born, how He died, why He died, and what He taught. The Gospels are a selected biography of Jesus Christ. The book of Acts relates the events of the early church and their response to Jesus and the gospel. It tells how they preached about Christ, and it includes some early sermons. It tells us how the church became the church. After a certain number of years, the story ends. The book of Acts stops just before the deaths of Peter and Paul.

Then we have the letters written by original apostles and those with apostolic authority, including Paul, James, and Jude, the half-brothers of Jesus. These letters give us eyewitness reports of what they saw and heard. With the death of John, the last living apostle, God's special revelation to humankind through humans ceased. God does not reveal Himself through prophets in this way anymore. There is still a prophetic gift, but it is different now. Technically, the prophetic gift today is illumination, not inspiration.

The beliefs of our LDS friends are difficult for us to understand. Of course, what we believe is not easy for them to understand either. When a person grows up hearing one thing all his or her life, it is difficult to understand something very different. The Mormons believe that the Bible is the word of God only where it is translated correctly. They cannot show any incorrect translation, but as I discussed earlier, they are not really talking about translation, but transmission. When Joseph Smith corrected the King James Version, he meant "this is what it should say," but he did not give any textual rationale for the change. He changed it with the authority of his prophetic office.

Our LDS friends believe that the Book of Mormon, *Doctrine and Covenants*, and *The Pearl of Great Price* are divinely inspired. The Mormon prophet Joseph Smith either wrote them, translated them from ancient documents, or recorded a received vision.

4

Who is GOD?

Is He an Exalted Man?

In normal conversation we won't notice much difference in our friend's words about God and our own. They talk of heavenly father very much in the way evangelicals do. However, the God who is behind the words looks like a very different god.

Robert Millet, professor of ancient scripture at Brigham Young University, admits that the LDS doctrine of God is a distinctive LDS doctrine.[22] Not only do they object strenuously to the Trinity, they also describe a God with a very different nature. Their idea of who God is and what God is like differs significantly from our understanding of the God of the Bible. The three things most noticeable are their belief that God is not spirit but that He has a physical body of flesh and bones, that God was not always God, but progressed to godhood, and that God is not the only god in existence.

God Has a Body of Flesh and Bones

In his chapter on God the Father, Millet revels in this distinction. "The latter-day Saints believe that God the Father is an exalted man, a corporeal being, a personage with flesh and bones. They do not believe he is a spirit, although they acknowledge that his spirit or sacred influence is everywhere present."[23] Here is the plain teaching that your Mormon friends and neighbors hear in their lessons and believe as the truth concerning God. Their lessons reinterpret verses that teach of God as Spirit to say something else. A good example of this is John 4:24. In this verse Jesus tells the woman at the well, "God *is* a Spirit: and they that worship him must worship *him* in spirit and in truth." To make this verse agree with the LDS teaching, the LDS church points to the Joseph Smith Translation of the Bible. David Ridges states, "Because John 4:24, as given in the bible, states that 'God is a Spirit,' many Christian religions have developed false teachings about the nature of God. Joseph Smith corrected this verse to read, 'For unto such hath God promised his Spirit. And they who worship him, must worship in spirit and in truth.'"[24] The only authority Joseph Smith had for changing the words and completely changing the meaning was his office as a prophet. He gave no manuscript evidence for making the changes or any reasons for the countless manuscripts in existence to be so wrong.

The Mormon God is God with a body of flesh and bones. This concept, of course, describes a very different God from the God in whom Evangelicals and other Christians believe and who is the object of their worship. The key to understanding this difference relates to our differing views of revelation as described in Chapter 1. Evangelicals believe that the Bible, from Genesis to Revelation, is the wholly inspired word of God. Hebrews 1 tells us the Bible is a complete testimony of God, who He is and what He has done. If someone comes with another teaching and we want to know if it is true, we look in the Bible, God's word, and ask, "What does the Bible teach?" The word for this is exegesis. Exegesis means that we study the Bible and out of that study, we determine our doctrine. We come to our beliefs from studying the word of God, the Bible.

Our LDS friends approach this from a different direction. They start with their doctrine of modern day prophets. Their core belief is that Joseph Smith was a prophet of God. In his office as prophet, Joseph Smith said some things about God, the church, etc., put them down in his writings, and gave those writings to the church to believe. Professor Millet explains this: "Though Latter-day Saints extensively use the scriptures to learn about God, their fundamental knowledge concerning him is based upon the Prophet Joseph Smith's first vision, the Prophet's subsequent revelatory experiences, and individual personal revelation."[25] Simply put, whatever Joseph Smith said, Mormons believe. "For Latter-day Saints, no theological or philosophical propositions about God can override the primary experience of the Prophet."[26] Having determined what Joseph Smith taught, they then go to the Bible to find proof it teaches the same thing. We have a term for that also: eisegesis.

Exegesis means to draw out. Eisegesis means to read in. The example above of Joseph Smith's revision of John 4:24 is a good example of eisegesis. Joseph Smith changed the passage by simply saying, "This is what that verse should say." He had no authority for changing it except his claim of being a prophet of God. All existing evidence verifies the reading in the Bible. Mormons, even LDS scholars, accept that Joseph Smith could override two thousand years of biblical scholarship and thousands of ancient manuscripts, without evidence of any kind, and change the words of Holy Scripture simply by saying, "God revealed to me. . . ."

The context of John 4 is the story of the woman at the well. Jesus comes to the well of Samaria, and a Samaritan woman is there. It is strange to her when he speaks to her because He is a Jew talking to a Samaritan and He is a man talking to a woman. He tells her who she is and the circumstances of her life. She is amazed that Jesus knows about her. They begin to have this discussion about living water. Unwilling to accept what He is saying, she tries to change the subject. "You are a Jew and you Jews believe that you have to worship God in Jerusalem. We are Samaritans and believe you worship God in the mountain of Samaria." In her understanding, the Jews believe God is in Jerusalem, and the Samaritans believe God is in Samaria.

Jesus patiently corrects her misunderstanding of God, explaining that He is in neither place. He tells her that God is Spirit and that He is not worshipped in the mountain; He is worshipped in spirit. It is not where a person is, but how he or she worships, that is the key element. Jesus' plain meaning is that God does not have a body with which we have to be in contact to worship Him; we can worship anywhere. He is Spirit and is as close to us as our worship. The very teaching of the passage is on the nature of God as Spirit and cannot be changed by altering one sentence.

Our LDS neighbors will explain God's physical body to us with Biblical texts that ascribe human traits to God. Exodus 33:11 is an example: "And the LORD spake unto Moses face to face, as a man speaketh unto his friend" (Exodus 33:11a). According to their understanding, since Moses saw the Lord face to face, then God must have a real face. If He has a real face, then He must have a whole physical body as well. Other passages our friends might reference are ones that talk about the hand of God or another body part. There are many of these references. Scholars call them anthropomorphisms. It is the act of giving God the characteristics of a man so that we can understand a concept. We understand "face to face" to mean God talked to Moses personally, or intimately. Moses was in the direct presence of God and interacted with Him on a personal and intimate basis.

Anthropomorphisms are one kind of metaphor. There are others. In Psalm 91 the psalmist gives God the characteristics of a mother bird to give us an image to which we can relate. "He shall cover you with his feathers, And under His wings shalt thou trust: His truth shall be thy shield and buckler" (Psalm 91:4). Obviously this verse doesn't mean that God's body includes wings and feathers. Nobody believes that. We may not know the correct term, but we understand this as metaphor. It is describing God with a characteristic to help us understand something about God. This beautiful metaphor gives us a picture of the refuge and the protection we find in God, just as a brood of chicks gather under their mother's wings.

Another reason Mormons believe God has a body like ours is the statement in Genesis that humankind is made in the image of God. If we are like God, then God is like us. Since we have a body of flesh and bones, God must have a body of flesh and bones since we are made in his image. This is a different concept of image than that of orthodox Christianity. We are different from all the rest of creation. The image of God means that we share in God's attributes, although not perfectly as He is. Those attributes are things like life, personality, truth, wisdom, love, holiness, justice. This image of God in us allows our spiritual fellowship with Him.

The Bible Teaches That God Is Invisible

Many verses teach that God is invisible. He is invisible because He is spirit.

"Now unto the King eternal, immortal, invisible, the only wise God, be honour and glory for ever and ever. Amen" (1 Timothy 1:17).

"Who is the image of the invisible God, the firstborn of every creature:" (Colossians 1:15).

"No man hath seen God at any time; the only begotten Son, which is in the bosom of the Father, he hath declared *him*" (John 1:18).

The gospel of John says that no one has ever seen God. The only explanation we have of God is Jesus Christ. In *Doctrine and Covenants* 84:19-22, that concept has been expanded to read that no man can see God without the authority of the priesthood. "Therefore, in the ordinances thereof, the power of godliness is manifest. And without the ordinances thereof, and the authority of the priesthood, the power of godliness is not manifest unto men in the flesh; for without this no man can see the face of God, even the Father, and live." Our Mormon neighbor may indeed believe that God is invisible to us. Because we do not have the LDS Priesthood, we have a lesser understanding of God.

It is the Christian's understanding that a God with a body of flesh and bones cannot be omnipresent. Body implies space, and a space occupying body cannot be but one place at a time. Omnipresence is one of our basic understandings about God. It is the belief that God is everywhere present all the time. The belief of Christendom has been as David prayed in the Psalm 139: "Where can I go to escape your presence." Since a body of flesh and bones can be in only one place at any time, the Latter Day Saint will admit that in their view, God is limited to one place at a time. They are quick to point out, however, that his influence is everywhere.

God Was Not Always God

A second major difference in our understanding of the nature of God is the Mormon belief that God was not always God, but that He progressed to become God. Our understanding of eternal is that God exists outside of time; He does not

45

progress in time. Since God created time, He must dwell outside of time and space, and He is not subject to either. Our LDS friends teach that there was a time when God was not God and that he eventually progressed to become God.

They do not believe God is eternal in the same way that we believe God is eternal. They do not believe that He is God in eternity past because there was a time in the past when He was not God. He began as mortal man, and after passing through a school of earth life similar to that through which we are now passing, He became God. The teachings that God is from everlasting to everlasting is explained by Mormon apologists as meaning that God has been around so long, so much longer than any of us, that it "seems" like He has been God from eternity past.

In the teachings of Joseph Smith, "God himself was once as we are now, and is an exalted man, and sits enthroned in yonder heavens."[27] According to Mormon belief, there was a time when God lived in a world like ours. He had a human body like ours, He had the opportunity to live according to gospel principles, and because He obeyed, He progressed to become God the father of our earth.

This is a major conflict with the evangelical understanding of God. We believe that God is eternal. He is God from all eternity. There are two basic existences. There is time and there is eternity. We all live in time, and everything we know, except God, is limited to time. God is not limited to time since He created it. He exists outside of time, in eternity. He is eternal. He is from everlasting to everlasting. He was God from all eternity past. He is God today, and He will remain God through all eternity future. He is always the same, never changing. The Bible speaks of his timelessness. "For I am the LORD, I change not; therefore ye sons of Jacob are not consumed" (Malachi 3:6)" Every good gift and every perfect gift is from above, and cometh down from the Father of lights, with whom is no variableness, neither shadow of turning" (James 1:17).

God is so stable that there is no variation in Him. If a person goes out in the morning, the shadow is to the west; if a person goes out in the afternoon, the shadow is to the east. That is a shifting shadow. James is saying that God is so stable that even His shadow never moves. He does not change. "They shall perish, but thou shalt endure: Yea, all of them shall wax old like a garment; As a vesture shalt thou change them, and they shall be changed: But thou *art* the same, And thy years shall have no end" (Psalm 102:26-27).

God is always the same. He does not change. People change, people perish, people wear out, but God is never changing. "Before the mountains were brought forth, or ever thou hadst formed the earth and the world, Even from everlasting to everlasting, thou art God" (Psalm 90:2). This eternality is what we believe about God. God has always been God. Before the creation of anything, God was already God. Before the beginning, God was God. Earlier Mormon works such as the Book of Mormon teach this same thing: "For I know that God is not a partial God, neither a changeable being; but he is unchangeable, from all eternity to all eternity" (Moroni 8:18). The same idea is reflected in Mormon 9:9-10. "For do we not read that God is the same yesterday, today, and forever, and in him there is no variableness neither shadow of changing? And now if ye have imagined up unto yourselves a God who doth vary, and in whom there is shadow of changing, then have ye imagined up unto yourselves a God who is not a God of miracles." With the modern revelation claimed by Joseph Smith, Mormons believe that instead of always being God, He has grown to become God.

There Are Other Gods Besides God

In addition to believing that God has not always been God and believing that He has a physical body of flesh and bones, our LDS friends also believe He is not the only God in existence. In worlds and universes beyond our understanding, there are other gods, although our God is the only God to whom we are subject. Bishop David Ridges, in his work on LDS doctrine, explains, "The scriptures teach that there are many people from other worlds who have already become gods. Many gods will be added in the universe when worthy mortals from this world become gods."[28]

Evangelicals believe that God is one. There is only one God, there has always been only one God, and there will always be only one God. Because of the LDS teaching that the Father, Son, and Holy Spirit are three separate Gods and because of their teaching that men may become gods, they believe there are more gods than one.

To help understand their theology of the oneness of God, Evangelicals can look at the very basic difference between the number one and every other number. If we have one, we have singular. If we have two, we have plural. If we have 200, 2,000, or 20,000,000, we have plural. If we have one, we have singular; any other number we have is plural. Over and over again the Bible teaches that God is singular: one. There is no plurality of Gods. All religions can be put into one of two classifications. There are those that are monotheistic. Mono means one. Theos means God. Three religions, Judaism, Islam, and Christianity, believe there is one God. Every other religion in history is polytheistic. Poly means more than one. Our LDS friends are polytheistic. They believe there is more than one God.

One Biblical passage Mormons will use to prove their doctrine is in Paul's first letter to the Corinthians: "For though there be that are called gods, whether in heaven or in earth, (as there be gods many, and lords many)" (1 Corinthians 8:5). This is a great example of eisegesis. If we look at the verse in context to understand Paul's teaching, we will read the verses before and after 8:5. That puts the passage in its context.

> As concerning therefore the eating of those things that are offered in sacrifice unto idols, we know that an idol *is* nothing in the world, and that *there is* none other God but one. For though there be that are called gods, whether in heaven or in earth, (as there be gods many, and lords many,) But to us *there is but* one God, the Father, of whom *are* all things, and we in him; and one Lord Jesus Christ, by whom *are* all things, and we by him (1 Corinthians 8:4-6).

Judaism accepted that the nations around them had their gods. However, they never accepted those gods as authentic. They were false gods. They were idols. The very core of Judaism that made them God's peculiar people was their belief in only one God.

Mormons believe there are three separate Gods in the Godhead; God the Father, God the Son, and God the Holy Ghost. These three Gods are one in eternal purpose. Most Mormons with whom I have discussed this concept misunderstand what we believe about the Godhead. They voice our doctrine by saying that we believe that God is three Gods in one person. Our actual belief is just opposite of that. We believe that there are three persons, but only one God. Somehow these three are united as one God. Is this hard to understand? Yes, it is hard to understand. The term we use to describe this three in one God is the Trinity.

Robert Millet describes the LDS teaching concerning the Godhead.

> Latter day saints worship God the Father, in the name of Christ the Son, by the power of the Holy Ghost. These three—Father, Son, and Holy Spirit—Constitute the Godhead. Latter day Saints believe that the members of the Godhead are three separate and distinct personages. Joseph Smith described them as "God the first, the Creator; God the second, the Redeemer; and God the third, the witness or Testator. The members of the Godhead are believed to be one in purpose, one in mind, one in glory, one in attributes and powers, but separate persons. Christ the Son and the Holy Spirit are subordinate beings to the Father, albeit divine beings, and partake of the attributes and powers of the Father.[29]

Conclusion

While we talk about God in many ways identical to our LDS friends, the God in whom we believe and about whom we talk is very different. One God is the God defined by traditional Christianity. Judaism and the Old Testament believe in one God. He has a long history and is defined in the Old and New Testaments of the Holy Bible. The Mormon god with a body is another god, a newer god, only about 200 years old, and is described by a self-proclaimed prophet.

      An understanding of the differences between Christianity's God and the Mormon God will aid us in understanding our Mormon friends and neighbors.

5
Who is Jesus Christ?

The Son of God or A Son of God

Our LDS friends and neighbors believe in Jesus Christ. Their belief is sincere and very meaningful to them. If asked about the relationship of Jesus Christ to their church, they will point to the church name, "The Church of Jesus Christ." They believe Jesus was a real person and that He is the Son of God and the Savior of the world. They claim to believe that Jesus is the only way to salvation. Today they proudly claim to be Christian and do not understand the current "Are Mormons Christian?" debate.

The key to this debate is the definition of Christian. In one sense Mormons are correct. Mormonism is certainly Christian rather than Buddhist or some other world religion. Mormonism falls under the realm of Christianity, not Islam, Hinduism, or Judaism. Mormon beliefs regarding Jesus are very similar to orthodox or evangelical beliefs. They speak of Him as being the living Lord, the focus of faith, the savior of the world, the son of God. "He is the Savior and the Redeemer of the world," testifies immediate past president and prophet of the LDS Church, Gordon Hinckley.[30]

The March 2008 issue of *Ensign Magazine*, a monthly periodical published by the LDS Church, is a special issue. The topic is "The Lord Jesus Christ." The whole issue consists of the teachings and testimony of LDS members concerning their belief in Jesus Christ. Probably close to 90% of the content would be acceptable in any Christian church. It is the other 10% that brings the accusation that Mormons are not Christian. When we delve deeper into their beliefs, we recognize that their understanding of Jesus is significantly different from evangelical, orthodox, or historic Christianity. Who is this Jesus on the masthead of their church? Who is it they follow? Is it the same Jesus described in the New Testament?

Jesus' Origin

For Mormons, Jesus is the firstborn spirit child of *Elohim* and Heavenly Mother. *The encyclopedia of Mormonism* contains this listing under "Premortal Jesus": "In the premortal life, Jesus Christ, whose main title was *Jehovah*, was the firstborn spirit child of God the Father and thus the eldest brother and preeminent above all other spirit children of God. In that First Estate, he came to be more intelligent than all other spirits, one 'like unto God.'"[31]

As I will discuss in the chapter on humankind, LDS belief is that before anyone came to live on this earth in the mortal state, they existed as preexistent spirits. Their dwelling place was in heaven with heavenly Father and Mother. All people are spirit children of these first parents. Jesus Christ was the first of those spirit children. We may hear our LDS neighbor or friend talk about Jesus as their elder brother. They believe that He is our elder spirit brother and that we are children of the same heavenly Mother and Father. Also born of this heavenly Mother and Father is Lucifer.

Heavenly Father and Heavenly Mother had many spirit children. Jesus was the first and the highest of their spirit children. The church's own *Encyclopedia of Mormonism* says this: "The first spirit born to our heavenly parents was Jesus Christ." *Doctrine and Covenants* says, "Christ, the firstborn, was the mightiest of all the spirit children of the Father." Their understanding is that Jesus is like us. He is just at a different degree. He is the mightiest, He is the eldest, but in essentials, He is like us.

Elohim and Jehovah

Elohim and *Jehovah*[32] are both names for God in the Old Testament. In a standard translation of the Bible, *Elohim* is usually translated "God" and *Jehovah* is translated "Lord," with the "ord" in small caps. The translators use this device to differentiate from *Adonai*, another Hebrew word for Lord. When the underlying word in the Hebrew text is *Adonai*, it is translated Lord, with regular letters.

Official LDS teaching is that *Elohim* is God the Father. When the Old Testament translates the word *Elohim*, it is speaking about God the Father. When the word is *Jehovah*, the reference is to Jesus. They believe Jesus is the *Jehovah* of the Old Testament.

> Since his premortal life, Jesus Christ has functioned as the constant associate of the Father working under his direction. In 1916 the First Presidency and the Quorum of the Twelve Apostles issued a doctrinal statement on the relationship between the Father and the Son: "Jesus the Son has represented and yet represents Elohim His Father in power and authority. This is true of Christ in His preexistent, antemortal, or unembodied state, in the which He was known as Jehovah; also during His embodiment in the flesh; and since that period in His resurrected state" (*MFP* 5:31-32). [33]

A careful reading of the Old Testament will show that does not work. There are a number of passages in the Old Testament where these two words, Elohim and Jehovah, obviously refer to the same person. For example, Genesis 27:20 says, "Isaac said to his son, 'How is it that you have it so quickly, my son?' And he said, 'Because the Lord your God caused it to happen to me.'" Using the Hebrew words as they appear in the text, the passage would say "because *Jehovah*, your *Elohim*, caused it to happen to me." Translating the words according to LDS understanding, the verse would say, "Jesus, your God the Father, caused it to happen to me."

Another example is in Exodus. In this passage God is speaking to Moses.

> He said also, "I am the God of your father, the God of Abraham, the God of Isaac, and the God of Jacob." Then Moses hid his face, for he was afraid to look at God. The Lord said, "I have surely seen the affliction of My people who are in Egypt, and have given heed to their cry because of their taskmasters, for I am aware of their sufferings (Exodus 3:6-7).

Using the Hebrew words the verse would read,

> He said also, "I am *Elohim* of your Father, *Elohim* of Abraham, *Elohim* of Isaac, and *Elohim* of Jacob." Then Moses hid his face for he was afraid to look at *Elohim*. Then *Jehovah* said, "I have surely seen the affliction of My people who are in Egypt, and have given heed to their cry because of their taskmasters, for I am aware of their sufferings."

The LDS translation then would be that *Jehovah* (Jesus) is speaking to them and saying, "I am God the father, I am the God the Father of Abraham, Isaac, Jacob, and I am *Jehovah* (Jesus)."

In Jeremiah 32:18 the prophet says, "Who shows lovingkindness to thousands, but repays the iniquity of fathers into the bosom of their children after them, O great and mighty God [Elohim]. [Jehovah] The Lord of hosts is His name;" The simple teaching of this verse is that it is God, *Elohim,* who shows lovingkindness. The Lord, *Jehovah,* is His name. What do the two names for God mean? *Elohim* is a generic word for God. It is not his name. It means "God." When the Bible talks about gods, including false gods, it uses the word *Elohim*. It is a word for God like we would use the generic word god. When God tells us His personal name, the name is *Jehovah*.

The Christmas prophecy of Isaiah 9:6 is a familiar passage: "For a child will be born to us, a son will be given to us; And the government will rest on His shoulders; And His name will be called Wonderful Counselor, Mighty (Elohim) God, Eternal Father, Prince of Peace." This verse is a prophecy of Jesus Christ. The prophet calls Jesus *Elohim* Himself, Mighty *Elohim*.

Deuteronomy 6:4 is a verse that is impressed upon every Jewish child. It says, "Hear, O Israel! The Lord is our God, the Lord is one!" Using the Hebrew words, it reads "Hear O Israel, *Jehovah* is our *Elohim*, *Jehovah* is one." We can see that this simply will not work using the definitions given in the *Encyclopedia of Mormonism*. In those terms, this verse would read "Hear O Israel, Jesus is our God the father, Jesus is one."

Orthodox Christians believe that *Elohim* is a generic word for God and that it is used in the Old Testament to mean God the Father. *Jehovah* is the personal name of God. Usually it refers to God the Father, but it can refer to God the Son. Since they are the same Triune God, there is no need to insist that it is one or the other.

The Story of Christmas

Our LDS friends and neighbors celebrate Christmas. Their celebration will be very similar to ours. When they tell the Christmas story, it is very likely there will be nothing different from our own celebration. Underneath the story, however, their understanding of the birth of Jesus is quite a departure from the Orthodox Christian understanding. Mormons teach that the conception of Jesus came in a physical relationship between *Elohim* and Mary. Remember that *Elohim* is a bodied god, known as God the Father. He has a body of flesh and bones, and the conjugal, physical relationship between God the Father or *Elohim* and Mary produced Jesus the son. Bruce McConkie explains,

> God the Father is a perfected, glorified, holy man, an immortal Personage. And Christ was born into the world as the literal Son of this Holy Being; he was born in the same personal, real, and literal sense that any mortal son is born to a mortal father. There is nothing figurative about his paternity; he was begotten, conceived, and born in the normal and natural course of events, for he is the Son of God, and that designation means what it says.[34]

Though he does not come right out and say it in plain English, we know what he means. We know how children are conceived. That is just what McConkie is saying. He is saying that Jesus was born of a physical relationship between God the Father and Mary. Ezra Taft Benson, a former prophet of the LDS Church, says the same thing, and then adds, "From Mary, a mortal woman, Jesus inherited mortality, including the capacity to die. From his exalted Father he inherited immortality, the capacity to live forever."[35] This is very different from the Bible's teaching that Jesus was immortal from the beginning. He did not inherit immortality from the Father. He was with God in the very beginning.

Benson says, "Jesus was not the son of Joseph, nor was He begotten by the Holy Ghost. He is the Son of the Eternal Father!"[36] This is very different from orthodox Christian belief. The gospels clearly teach that Jesus was conceived by the Holy Ghost (Spirit). "Now the birth of Jesus Christ was on this wise: When as his mother Mary was espoused to Joseph, before they came together, she was found with child of the Holy Ghost" (Matthew 1:18). Then we are told of Joseph's angelic encounter: "But while he thought on these things, behold, the angel of the Lord appeared unto him in a dream, saying, Joseph, thou son of David, fear not to take unto thee Mary thy wife: for that which is conceived in her is of the Holy Ghost" (Matthew 1:20). This Spirit conception is further confirmed by the angel's words to Mary: "Then said Mary unto the angel, How shall this be, seeing I know not a man? And the angel answered and said unto her, The Holy Ghost shall come upon thee, and the power of the Highest shall overshadow thee: therefore also that holy thing which shall be born of thee shall be called the Son of God" (Luke 1:34-35).

Mary asked the angel, "How can this be since I am a virgin?" If she had had sex with a physical being, even if the physical being was a "god," she would not have had to ask that question. The LDS teaching is that she remained a virgin because she had sex with an immortal being, not with a mortal being. Even though this immortal partner had a body of flesh and bones, she remained a virgin. Mary had physical sex with *Elohim*, an immortal man with a body of flesh and bones, but she was still considered a virgin because she had not had sex with a mortal man.

The orthodox view is that Mary did not even have sex with the Holy Spirit but that in some miraculous way, the Holy Spirit implanted the child into Mary to provide his human existence. Human methods cannot explain it, nor was it meant to be explained.

For our Mormon friend, the words of scripture, even the words of the Bible as they describe the most holy Christmas event, the virgin birth of Jesus Christ, are secondary to the new revelations given to the prophets. Thus Benson can completely contradicted the Bible while appealing to new and continuing revelation. Our LDS neighbor has no problem with this. "That is the advantage," he might say, "of having a living prophet."

Everlasting to Everlasting

The historic Christian belief related to an eternal Jesus is different from the belief of our Mormon friends. We believe that Jesus is coeternal, always existing with the Father. He is from eternity past and was with the Father in the beginning. Jesus has always existed. There was never a time that Jesus did not already exist. He is eternal as is God the Father. "In the beginning was the Word, and the Word was with God, and the Word was God. The same was in the beginning with God. All things were made by him; and without him was not any thing made that was made" (John 1:1-3). That John intended us to understand that the Word was Jesus is plainly seen in John 1:14, where he says, "And the word became flesh and dwelt among us." This is the beginning of John's story about Jesus. Jesus is from the very beginning.

The Book of Mormon uses eternity to eternity to talk about Jesus. Mosiah 3:5, 8 in the Book of Mormon says that Jesus is both from eternity to eternity and the creator of all things. BYU professor Robert Millet tries to explain this in his book, *The Mormon Faith*. Speaking of Heavenly Father, he says, "Because he has held his exalted status for a longer period than any of us can conceive, he is able to speak in terms of eternity and can state that he is from everlasting to everlasting." [37]

In other words, even though he is not from eternity to eternity, he is from so long ago we do not know the difference. Then Millet quotes Joseph Fielding Smith,

> From eternity to eternity means from the spirit existence through the probation which we are in, and then back again to the eternal existence which will follow. Surely this is everlasting, for when we receive the resurrection, we say of myself and others, we

are from eternity; and we will be to eternity everlasting, if we receive the exaltation. [38]

He says, "If we receive the exultation," which is their word for going through the steps of salvation, then we too will be known as "being from eternity to eternity." According to Mormons, the difference between Jesus Christ and ourselves is not so much one of a different existence, with one being God and one being creature, one being eternal and one being mortal, one being worthy and one being like us; it is simply a matter of degree. We are almost, or could be almost, like Jesus and eventually could be like Jesus. In the Bible nothing could be less true. Jesus is totally different from us. He is from all eternity, meaning that He was in the beginning with God. It is not even that He was created at the beginning; He was the creator. "For by him were all things created, that are in heaven, and that are in earth, visible and invisible, whether *they be* thrones, or dominions, or principalities, or powers: all things were created by him, and for him" (Colossians 1:16).

In the context of this verse, Paul clearly says Jesus Christ created all things. He does not leave the reader in the dark as to what he means by "all things." Paul goes on to say that everything that's in heaven and everything that's on earth was created by Jesus. He further clarifies by saying Jesus Christ created everything that's visible and everything that's invisible. Then he adds, "Whether thrones, dominions, or rulers or authorities, all things have been created through Him and for Him." The words thrones, dominions, rulers, and authorities are classes of angelic beings in Jewish theology.

The teaching of the Bible is not that Jesus is Satan's older brother, but that Jesus created Satan as one of the angels. He is the Creator of Satan, not His spirit brother, and He is our Creator, not our spirit brother, not our elder brother. He is our Creator.

Conclusion

A cursory look at LDS beliefs about Jesus will show them to be very much the same as ours. They use many of the same words, scriptures, and teachings. Some of the differences are hidden from view, either intentionally or innocently.

Paul was concerned that his followers not be deceived as to who Jesus is. He warned the church at Corinth,

> But I fear, lest by any means, as the serpent beguiled Eve through his subtilty, so your minds should be corrupted from the simplicity that is in Christ. For if he that cometh preacheth another Jesus, whom we have not preached, or *if* ye receive another spirit, which ye have not received, or another gospel, which ye have not accepted, ye might well bear with *him* (2 Corinthians 11:3-4).

Paul is talking about those that have come into Corinth to try to lead them astray in exactly this way. These interlopers are preaching a different spirit, a different Jesus, and a different gospel.

What if the Jesus preached is a different Jesus? To preach another Jesus would not be truth. It would not be valid to teach another Jesus. When our Mormon friends say, "We believe in Jesus of Nazareth, we believe Him to be the Son of God and the Savior or the world, we take upon ourselves the name Christian and are counted among his followers. We believe that Jesus Christ is the one and only route to salvation; therefore, are not we the same?"

How do we answer? What if the Jesus is not the same Jesus? What if we are not talking about the same God and the same gospel?

They believe Jesus is the Firstborn spirit child of *Elohim* and Heavenly Mother. Other spirit children include each of us and our other brother, Satan. Orthodox Christians, on the other hand, believe that Jesus is coeternal with the Father and has always existed. Our Mormon neighbor believes that Jesus was conceived in a physical relationship between *Elohim* and Mary. Orthodoxy teaches that Jesus was conceived supernaturally by the Holy Spirit.

Their belief is that Jesus earned his own salvation by the works that He did. We believe that Jesus needed no salvation. I will explore this further in the next chapter on the Gospel.

Are we talking about the same Jesus? Does it make any difference? Paul thought it did, even to the point of blaming the different Jesus on Satan himself. "For such *are* false apostles, deceitful workers, transforming themselves into the apostles of Christ. And no marvel; for Satan himself is transformed into an angel of light" (2 Corinthians 11:13-14).

6

Salvation and the Gospel

How Do We Become Right With God?

The essential question of evangelical Christianity is not so much how did we get here, or even who God is, or what do we believe about the Trinity, but how do we reach eternity? In the words of the Philippian jailer, "What must I do to be saved?" (Acts 16:30). This is the essence of the differences between Evangelicals and Mormons.

The gospel answers the question of salvation. Jesus Christ died for our sins, and on the third day He rose from the dead. He offers forgiveness of sins to all who believe and trust in Him. With this forgiveness, we receive eternal life.

My introduction to the Mormon usage of the word Gospel came in my first few weeks in Utah. I was observing an encounter with some LDS missionaries. Some new friends, thinking I needed the LDS education if I was going to live and minister in Utah, accepted a request from LDS missionaries to receive the first lesson, and they invited me to attend as an observer. After sitting quietly through the whole presentation, the lead missionary sought my response to what I had heard.

My response came in the form of a quote from the New Testament: "But though we, or an angel from heaven, preach any other gospel unto you than that which we have preached unto you, let him be accursed" (Galatians 1:8). I was certain I had just heard a different Gospel than the one preached by the first century apostles, abundantly found throughout the New Testament. The missionary's response totally floored me. He quoted from Ephesians 4:11, "And He personally gave some to be apostles, some prophets, some evangelists, some pastors and teachers" (HCSB). He then explained the gospel to me this way. "We are the only church that has apostles and prophets today, so we are the correct church. This is the gospel Paul preached." Obviously, we have a difference of opinion about the Gospel.

What Your Mormon Friends and Neighbors Believe

When a Mormon is baptized at age 8, she believes she is making a public stance for Jesus Christ. She is making the promise to be faithful to the Lord, to the Church, and to her decision. Worthy priesthood members and members of her own family observe this commitment. She has now accepted the atonement of Christ for herself, and the only thing left for her to do is to live her life in a worthy manner. She has free agency and her eternal future is now up to her. If she does well enough, she will someday return to the celestial kingdom of her heavenly parents. (See Appendix VII)

The Mormon plan of salvation, while containing many of the same words as that of Evangelicals, is very different. They begin with their belief that we are all spirit children of Heavenly Father and Heavenly Mother. We existed as spirits in a heavenly realm before we were born into an earthly family. The Father's plan is to get us home again. If we listen to our friends carefully, we will hear them talk of returning to Heavenly Father, or to Heavenly Father's house, but not of going to heaven.

In their belief, God created this earth so we would receive a body. At the same time, a veil drawn between heaven and earth keeps us from any memory of our prior existence. Thus we are required to live in this mortal existence by faith. In order to dwell in the highest degree of heaven, we have to earn our way on this earth through our own faith and behavior. This life is one of probation to see if we can qualify for the highest level of heaven. According to former LDS bishop W. F. Walker Johanson, "To Mormons, this is the reason the earth exists. They believe that everyone will be resurrected through Christ's Resurrection, but qualification for the highest level of glory in the Celestial Kingdom of heaven is based on their behavior while on the earth."[39] (See Appendix VII)

Because of the atonement of Jesus Christ, which He accomplished in the garden of Gethsemane, and his resurrection from the dead, all humankind will be resurrected. The Mormons call this immortality. For them, however, each individual will be judged according to how well he or she lived on the earth. If someone had opportunity to hear the principles of the Gospel, and by that they mean Mormonism, then that person will be judged according to how well he or she lived the principles.

The atonement makes it possible for those who have faith in Christ to be saved from their sins. Yet Mormons must do their part. That part is defined as repent, be baptized by one having authority, receive the Holy Ghost, and obey his commandments. So the death of Christ did not forgive anyone's sins; again, it only made possible the forgiveness of sins by law keeping. They further believe that if a person lived before the restoration of the gospel or died without knowing the principles, they will be judged according to how well they lived the golden rule. If they lived good enough, at some point some present or future day Mormon will be baptized for them by proxy in a Mormon temple, thus qualifying them to return to heavenly parents.

Grace

In a discussion with our friends and neighbors we will be tempted to present the divine doctrine of Salvation by Grace. They will be impressed because their gospel is obviously a gospel of works, not grace. Our friends have a doctrine of grace, radically redefining grace, but they are comfortable with it. Bishop Johanson explains grace: "Mormons believe that Jesus' resurrection is a free gift to all, but that His Atonement for their sins can only be accessed through faith in His name, sincere repentance, Baptism by one having authority, and the Holy Ghost. . . all of which provide a way for people to have their sins forgiven, if they repent."[40]

Mormons define grace as the chance to be forgiven if we live a good enough life, and they believe that a person's own behavior will be the determining factor in where he or she will be assigned for eternity. Without grace no one could make it, but grace only presents the opportunity. The *Mormon Encyclopedia* makes this salvation by works very clear:

> We accept Christ's atonement by placing our faith in him. Through this faith, we repent of

our sins, are baptized, receive the Holy Ghost, and obey his commandments. We become faithful disciples of Jesus Christ. The atonement makes it possible to be saved from sin if we do our part.[41]

To understand this works theology, it is necessary to define certain terms. LDS Church Apostle Elder M. Russell Ballard in a talk about the simple gospel, explains the meaning of faith. "Do you serve God, show kindness to others, pray, read scriptures, avoid pornography, participate in church meetings, and are 'preparing for and actively pursuing finding your eternal companion?'"[42]

The *Encyclopedia of Mormonism* says of repentance: "Before a person can be forgiven their sins they must repent." Then they define repentance as consisting of seven elements.

1. We Must Recognize Our Sins
2. We Must Feel Sorrow for Our Sins.
3. We Must Forsake Our Sins.
4. We Must Confess Our Sins.
5. We Must Make Restitution.
6. We Must Forgive others.
7. We Must Keep the Commandments of God.[43]

The encyclopedia explains each of these further. Confession of sins includes confessing them to the Lord and confessing more serious sins to the proper priesthood authority. Keeping the commandments involves paying tithes, keeping the Sabbath day, obeying the Word of Wisdom, sustaining the authorities of the church, loving the Lord, loving humanity, consistently saying family prayers, etc. Repentance involves all this and then spending the balance of one's life trying to live the commandments of the Lord so He can eventually pardon and cleanse the person. In other words, a Mormon's sins are not forgiven at all until all of this is accomplished.

Ensign Magazine, a publication of the LDS Church, makes this clear.

For example, while all members of the human family are freely given a reprieve from Adams's sin through no effort of their own, they are not given a reprieve from their own sins unless they pledge faith in Christ, repent of those sins, are baptized in His name, receive the gift of the Holy Ghost and confirmation into Christ's Church, and press forward in faithful endurance the remainder of life's journey.[44]

[margin note: WORKS Righteousness]

Though our LDS friends and neighbors will tell us they believe in Salvation by Grace, they have defined both salvation and grace differently. They have a salvation by works theology. Mormon theologians use words to define it as salvation by grace, but only by redefining grace and salvation.

The Teaching of Evangelical Christianity

If all of this sounds technical and complicated, it is, because, like most religions, Mormonism is heavy with rules and regulations. The evangelical Christian believes that salvation comes by faith. That faith is by itself; it is not faith plus anything. It is faith alone. Jesus' atonement provides for the forgiveness of sin by faith. That faith is faith in Jesus Christ alone. It is not faith in Jesus Christ plus faith in a prophet, a church, a system, or any other thing. The atonement of Jesus Christ is sufficient by itself to purchase salvation. Salvation is faith alone in Jesus Christ alone by Grace alone. The definition of Grace is "free gift."

God made the gospel simple. Humankind searching for God complicates it. Having seven steps of repentance followed by numerous definitions of commandment keeping and even then not being assured of success is the human way. A simple grace, appropriated by faith, is God's way.

In the book of Acts, a man asks the apostle Paul the same question with which we began this chapter. What must I do to be saved? Look how Paul answered.

> Who, having received such a charge, thrust them into the inner prison, and made their

feet fast in the stocks. And at midnight Paul and Silas prayed, and sang praises unto God: and the prisoners heard them. And suddenly there was a great earthquake, so that the foundations of the prison were shaken: and immediately all the doors were opened, and every one's bands were loosed. And the keeper of the prison awaking out of his sleep, and seeing the prison doors open, he drew out his sword, and would have killed himself, supposing that the prisoners had been fled. But Paul cried with a loud voice, saying, Do thyself no harm: for we are all here. Then he called for a light, and sprang in, and came trembling, and fell down before Paul and Silas, And brought them out, and said, Sirs, what must I do to be saved? And they said, Believe on the Lord Jesus Christ, and thou shalt be saved, and thy house (Acts 16:24-31).

[margin note: Also: Thief on the cross.]

The Philippian jailer asked Paul, "What must I do to be saved?" In his answer Paul said nothing about requiring baptism by one with the authority of the priesthood. He didn't tell the jailer he must receive the gift of the Holy Ghost and keep the commandments. He didn't encourage him to work his way to the celestial kingdom. Paul's response was much simpler. "Believe in the Lord Jesus, and you will be saved," Obviously Paul didn't believe the other things necessary. He lived in the time of the original gospel, not the restored gospel, and all those steps were foreign to him.

If a seeker invited us to come to his or her home because he or she wanted to investigate our religion, what would we say? Do we know? I am hoping we would tell the seeker about the Love of God who sent his only begotten Son into the world. We should say that Jesus died on the cross as payment for sin. We would then invite that person to accept Jesus Christ as Lord and Savior.

When Mormon missionaries go into a home, they talk about Joseph Smith, the Mormon Church, the restoration of the priesthood, and eternal families. The book of Acts tells the story of when Peter had the opportunity to go into a home and share the gospel. Look at what he told the family there.

Send therefore to Joppa, and call hither Simon, whose surname is Peter; he is lodged in the house of *one* Simon a tanner by the sea side: who, when he cometh, shall speak unto thee. Immediately therefore I sent to thee; and thou hast well done that thou art come. Now therefore are we all here present before God, to hear all things that are commanded thee of God. Then Peter opened *his* mouth, and said, Of a truth I perceive that God is no respecter of persons: But in every nation he that feareth him, and worketh righteousness, is accepted with him. The word which *God* sent unto the children of Israel, preaching peace by Jesus Christ: (he is Lord of all:) That word, *I say*, ye know, which was published throughout all Judaea, and began from Galilee, after the baptism which John preached; How God anointed Jesus of Nazareth with the Holy Ghost and with power: who went about doing good, and healing all that were oppressed of the devil; for God was with him. And we are witnesses of all things which he did both in the land of the Jews, and in Jerusalem; whom they slew and hanged on a tree: Him God raised up the third day, and shewed him openly; Not to all the people, but unto witnesses chosen before of God, *even* to us, who did eat and drink with him after he rose from the dead. And he commanded us to preach unto the people, and to testify that it is he which was ordained of God *to be* the Judge of quick and dead. To him give all the prophets witness, that through his name whosoever believeth in him shall receive remission of sins. While Peter yet spake these words, the Holy Ghost fell on all them which heard the word (Acts 10:32-44).

In summary, here is what he told them.

      v34 God's is the God of any who will receive Him.

      v36 Jesus Christ is Lord of all

      v38 We witnessed his perfect life

      v39 They killed him on a cross

      v40 He arose on the third day

> v43 Through his name everyone who believes in Him receives forgiveness of sins.

There is no mention of a church, a priesthood, a laying on of hands, a step to different kingdoms. It is just a simple "believe in the Lord Jesus Christ."

Examining the Difference

People who follow a works theology accuse those of us who have a grace theology of being soft on sin. They claim that the simple gospel of grace teaches that people can live however they want as long as they believe, or at least say the prayer and confess belief in Jesus. I am always thankful when I am accused of that because my tendency, just like the tendency of all who live in their humanness, is to become legalistic and works oriented. I praise the Lord when I am accused of being too easy on sinners because then I am being accused just as Jesus was accused.

Of course, the accusation is not correct. We do not teach that at all. We believe when a person truly accepts Jesus Christ as Lord, when that person totally trusts Christ, he is converted. In the authentic conversion experience, there is a change of heart, a new person who begins to live for Jesus. The conversion comes first though, by grace through faith.

The Divine Atonement

For the LDS member, The Divine Atonement best describes the work of Christ. The atonement took place in the garden of Gethsemane when Jesus took the sins and ills of the world on Himself and suffered there for them. In so doing, He paid the penalty for Adam's sin. This gives every human the opportunity to be forgiven of sin. Now that the sin of Adam is taken care of, the only sin individuals are responsible for is their own sin. By repentance and faithfulness one can now have the opportunity to be forgiven.

Faithfulness means an individual will be an active participating member of the Church of Jesus Christ of Latter-day Saints. He or she will be baptized by them and receive the priesthood if the person is a male. The new church member will attend the quorum meetings, take the sacrament weekly, pay a tithe, find and marry his or her eternal companion, respond to the church's call for a two year mission, etc.

Mormons are sure their commitments to their church and their good works are what are necessary for them to make their way back to the heavenly father. Grace? Yes Grace is necessary, but it is only valid after they have done all they can do on their own. This is human religion. All earthly religions teach some form of good works. We have to work hard to please the gods, and maybe they will see fit to find us worthy. True Christianity is just the opposite. God, in Jesus Christ, already did all the work. He just wants us to trust him for our salvation. This is a different gospel.

7

Humankind

Who Am I and Where Did I come From?

Our Mormon friend or neighbor has different beliefs than us regarding life, where they came from, who they are, and where they are going. The principle of eternal progression is fundamental to the LDS worldview. Having said that, the specifics of this progression are sometimes hard to ascertain. Even recent prophet of the LDS church Gordon Hinckley admits to some difficulty understanding it.

The *Encyclopedia of Mormonism* recognizes the problem: "The principle of eternal progression cannot be precisely defined or comprehended, yet it is fundamental to the LDS worldview."[45]

[Handwritten margin note: So why not extend the same to our view of Trinity.]

Three Estates

The basic LDS teaching is that humans have three successive estates of existence. The first estate was in the past when the individual was a spirit being living with heavenly father and mother. LDS members believe that they were born in heaven as spiritual children of these spiritual parents. They address this heavenly father in prayer. They profess to worship him, and eventually they will be like this heavenly being. We may hear evidence of this belief in statements our friends make about "returning to heavenly father," or "to heavenly father's house."

Living on earth is the second estate. The first estate spirit beings are born on earth, receiving a body of flesh. Every baby born on earth provides a body of flesh for a pre-existent spirit to enter into for the second estate. In the second estate there is no remembrance of the previous spiritual existence because of a veil placed between earth and the first estate. The second estate is a time of testing and probation. Those who pass the test of the second estate will be worthy to receive exaltation in the next life.

Mormon families believe the more children they have, the greater the number of spirits who will have the opportunity to be raised in LDS homes. The opportunity for these spirits to succeed in the second estate and achieve exaltation is likewise increased. This belief historically is the basis for Mormon couples to have many children.

This is also the origin of the belief that Jesus and Satan are brothers. All humans on earth are pre-existent brothers and sisters, born of the same heavenly father and mother. Jesus was the first-born. Satan was next. There was a contest between them for determining the plan of salvation. Satan wanted to force salvation on everyone, taking away freedom of choice. Jesus volunteered to give his life as payment for sin and to provide atonement of all. He set no plan or conditions of his own but said, "Father, thy will be done, and the glory be thine forever." Heavenly father chose Jesus' plan.[46]

Progression to and in the third estate is the perplexing belief. In my research on the doctrine, I found some books by Mormon authors that teach that God was once a man on another earthlike planet. There he died, was resurrected, and progressed to godhood of this planet where He and his heavenly wives produce the spirit children who are all their spirit brothers and sisters, including Jesus and Satan. Our neighbor or friend may believe parts of this less confidently. The *Encyclopedia of Mormonism* is more confident than the prophet on this subject. "Latter-day Saints believe that God achieved his exalted rank by progressing much as man must progress and that God is a perfected and exalted man:"[47] Our Mormon friend or neighbor may or may not understand God in this way. He may not believe men can become a god. There seems to be some room to maneuver in current Mormon theology. They do believe that this life is the second estate and the second step on the way to their own exaltation.

The official position of the church is that although this is a fundamental doctrine, it cannot be precisely defined or comprehended. In public appearances in the late 90s, then LDS Church President/Prophet/Seer/Revelator Gordon Hinckley evaded the question about God once being a man. From the top down, Mormon scholars debate exactly what this doctrine means. In its April 13, 1997, edition, the San Francisco Chronicle quoted President Hinckley's comments about this exaltation.

> SFC: There are some significant differences in your beliefs. For instance, don't Mormons believe that God was once a man?
>
> GBH: I wouldn't say that. There was a little couplet coined, ``As man is, God once was. As God is, man may become.'' Now that's more of a couplet than anything else. That gets into some pretty deep theology that we don't know very much about.
>
> SFC: So you're saying the church is still struggling to understand this?
>
> GBH: Well, as God is, man may become. We believe in eternal progression. Very strongly. We believe that the glory of God is intelligence and whatever principle of intelligence we attain unto in this life, it will rise with us in the Resurrection. Knowledge, learning, is an eternal thing. And for that reason, we stress education. We're trying to do all we can to make of our people the ablest, best, brightest people that we can. [48]

In August of that same year, in an interview with *Time Magazine,* President Hinckley answered this way.

> TIME: Just another related question that comes up is the statements in the King Follet discourse by the Prophet.
>
> GBH: Yeah
>
> TIME: ... about that, God the Father was once a man as we were. This is something that Christian writers are always addressing. Is this the teaching of the church today, that God the Father was once a man like we are?
>
> GBH: I don't know that we teach it. I don't know that we emphasize it. I haven't heard it discussed for a long time in public discourse. I

don't know. I don't know all the circumstances under which that statement was made. I understand the philosophical background behind it. But I don't know a lot about it and I don't know that others know a lot about it.[49]

After drawing quite a few negative comments from LDS sources, President Hinckley, speaking in the 1997 October General Conference, said,

I personally have been much quoted, and in a few instances misquoted and misunderstood. I think that's to be expected. None of you need worry because you read something that was incompletely reported. You need not worry that I do not understand some matters of doctrine. I think I understand them thoroughly, and it is unfortunate that the reporting may not make this clear. I hope you will never look to the public press as the authority on the doctrines of the Church.[50]

These examples leave room for some doubt among our LDS friends and neighbors on what they believe about these things. They will agree that the goal for church members is to live well in the second estate so they can experience the principles of exaltation. *Gospel Principles,* which is published by the Church of Jesus Christ of Latter-day Saints, explains the blessings of exaltation.

1. They will live eternally in the presence of Heavenly Father and Jesus Christ.
2. They will become gods.
3. They will have their righteous family members with them and will be able to have spirit children also. These spirit children will have the same relationship to them as we do to our Heavenly Father. They will be an eternal family.
4. They will receive a fullness of joy.
5. They will have everything that our Heavenly Father and Jesus Christ have—

all power, glory, dominion, and knowledge. [51]

Blessing numbers 3 and 5 give each Mormon the hope of one day being Heavenly Father just as Heavenly Father today is God in heaven. They believe they can be gods of their own planet. The requirements for gaining such a high exaltation are not easy, and many of our friends and neighbors will realize that godhood is beyond their reach. They do still believe that it is possible that many of their more righteous church members will make it.

Gospel Principles is specific about the requirements for exaltation. "To be exalted, we first must place our faith in Jesus Christ and then endure in that faith to the end of our lives. Our faith in him must be such that we repent of our sins and obey his commandments."[52] Following that statement are twenty-one specific commandments. Four of them are LDS ordinances.

1. Be baptized and confirmed as a member of the LDS church.
2. Receive the gift of the Holy Ghost by the laying on of hands.
3. Receive the temple endowment.
4. Be married for time and eternity.

The other seventeen include some of the Ten Commandments and general Christian characteristics, the "love thy neighbor," kind of requirements. They also include tithing, obeying the word of wisdom, searching ancestry and performing ordinances for them, attending church meetings, and listening to and obeying the inspired words of the prophets of the Lord (see Appendix II).

Joseph Smith taught that these are the steps that God went through in order to become God, and our Mormon friends believe in them.

This is the way our Heavenly Father became God. Joseph Smith taught: "It is the first principle of the Gospel to know for a certainty the character of God. . . . <u>He was once a man like us;</u> . . . God himself, the Father of us all, <u>dwelt</u> on an earth, the same as Jesus Christ himself did" (Teachings of the Prophet Joseph Smith, pp. 345-46).[53]

Christian Teachings about Godhood

Mormon apologists often point to statements made by Christian scholars and theologians about men becoming like God, or Godlike. For example, BYU professor Robert Millet in his book, *The Mormon Faith,* says this.

> Q. Do the Mormons really believe that men and women can become gods? Are they then polytheists?
>
> Latter-day Saints believe that we come to the earth to take a physical body, to be schooled and trained and gain experiences here that we could not have in the premortal life, and then to seek to grow in faith and spiritual graces until we can qualify to go where God and Christ are. But they believe that eternal life consists in more than being *with* (emphasis in original) God; it entails being *like* God. A study of the Christian church reveals that the doctrine of the deification of man was taught at least into the fifth century by such notables as Irenaeus, Clement of Alexandria, Justin Martyr, Athanasius, and Augustine.[54]

Another BYU Professor, Stephen Robinson, in his book *Are Mormons Christians,* quotes these early Christians as well as C. S. Lewis and likens the LDS belief in becoming gods to their quotes on our being "Like God," or on being "sons of God," or "joint heirs with Christ." He further points to the belief that we will have some God-like duties in the world to come. Then he states that this is the same as the LDS doctrine.

<u>There is a major difference that they are either missing or deliberately misrepresenting.</u> All of these early church fathers and C. S. Lewis believed that the difference between God and

men is a difference in kind. God's existence is a different kind of existence than human existence. God is God. He was always God and He will always be God. This God created humans, and humans will always be created. We may become like God, as the church fathers say, meaning we can grow and mature to achieve some of his characteristics: love, kindness, etc. Jesus said our goal is to become perfect, as God is perfect. No matter how much we mature, we will always be creation and God will always be God. Mormons, on the other hand, believe the difference between God and men is one of degree. He was once like us, but has progressed to become God. We are like He was, but are progressing to be like He is. These two beliefs are not the same.

Proof of Pre-existence

Our LDS friends might use certain scriptures to prove people exist as spirits before they are born. For example, the Old Testament prophet Jeremiah wrote, "Before I formed thee in the belly I knew thee; and before thou camest forth out of the womb I sanctified thee, *and* I ordained thee a prophet unto the nations" (Jeremiah 1:5).

LeGrande Richards, a former Mormon Apostle, says that this verse firmly establishes the preexistence of Jeremiah. He says it is proof that "we all lived in the spirit before we were born in the flesh. . . Jeremiah could not have been so called and ordained before he was born if he did not exist."[55] Richards' statement is true only if one has the LDS limited view of the omnipotence of God. The Biblical God is absolutely sovereign, eternal, outside of time and space, and He is all-knowing, all powerful, and everywhere-present. He knows us before we exist.

Jesus' preexistence is another proof Mormons use. For example, in the Gospel of John Jesus prayed, "And now, O Father, glorify thou me with thine own self with the glory which I had with thee before the world was" (John 17:5). We Evangelicals do believe that Jesus preexisted, but we also believe that Jesus is eternal God, God in the flesh. Since God is God from eternity to eternity, He truly existed before he was born. The incarnation is when Jesus emptied himself of his

77

divinity and took on flesh when He was born to Mary in a Bethlehem stable. We are creation, not eternal, and thus we are not like Jesus in this at all.

The New Testament teaches us that we are not born children of God. We become his children through the new birth.

> For ye have not received the spirit of bondage again to fear; but ye have received the Spirit of adoption, whereby we cry, Abba, Father. The Spirit itself beareth witness with our spirit, that we are the children of God: And if children, then heirs; heirs of God, and joint-heirs with Christ; if so be that we suffer with *him*, that we may be also glorified together (Romans 8:15-17).

Also, John 1:12 says, "But as many as received him, to them gave he power to become the sons of God, *even* to them that believe on his name:" Finally, God created man, not procreated man. "I have made the earth, the man and the beast that *are* upon the ground, by my great power and by my outstretched arm, and have given it unto whom it seemed meet unto me" (Jeremiah 27:5). This idea is further seen in Genesis 2:7: "And the LORD God formed man *of* the dust of the ground, and breathed into his nostrils the breath of life; and man became a living soul."

Paul clearly states that in order of appearance, the natural appears before the spiritual. We were physical beings before we were spiritual beings, not the other way around. "Howbeit that *was* not first which is spiritual, but that which is natural; and afterward that which is spiritual" (1 Corinthians 15:46).

Conclusion

Two of the foundational questions of life are "Where did I come from?" and "Where am I going?" The answers any person gives to those questions are essential to a worldview. Our Mormon friends have different answers to both. At the very basis of who we are as people, we disagree on our human nature.

8

Temples and Ordinances

Does God Live in a House?

Temples are very important to our Mormon friends. From a very young age their families and teachers tell them that these structures are more than simple buildings. They are the "house of the Lord." Many of them grew up in a home where a picture of a temple held a prominent place. Mormons are encouraged to have such a picture and to teach their children continually about the purpose of the house of the Lord.

If they grew up in an LDS family, their parents taught that they someday they would be able to enter the temple. Parents and church leaders told them of its delights and its beauty. Older siblings and cousins spoke of temples with a sense of reverence and awe. They saw older family members go to the house of the Lord, but for them it was sacred and unavailable until they were older. Parents and teachers constantly reminded them that temples are one thing that makes the Church of Jesus Christ of Latter Day Saints special and unique. Other churches don't have them because God revealed them in this last day to Joseph Smith and the prophets who followed him.

Before the Church dedicates a new temple, or rededicates a remodeled one, the temples are open to the public for tours. They show the rooms, the photos, and the baptismal font, and they make an effort to explain them to the non-member. Then there is a dedication ceremony and the temple becomes the house of the Lord, vested with a character so sacred that only members of the Church in good standing are permitted to enter. Mormons claim that the closed temple and the ceremonies that occur within are not secret; they are just so sanctified that it is wrong to even talk of them outside the walls of the Temple.

Most LDS people talk about temples in reverent tones. They are very proud of them and are offended if anyone says anything negative about them. It is almost as bad as blaspheming God Himself. When a new temple is opened anywhere in the world, it is a Utah news item. The event is reported about in the paper and seen on every TV news channel. Every April and October when the church meets for its semiannual conference, a report is given on the current number of existing temples, on how many new temples have opened since the last conference, and of any plans for new ones.

For those of us outside Mormonism, this reverence for temples is hard to understand. For the Latter-day Saint, however, the temple has a very important religious purpose. Former Church President Howard W. Hunter writes, "All our efforts in proclaiming the gospel, perfecting the Saints, and redeeming the dead lead to the holy temple. This is because the temple ordinances are absolutely crucial; we cannot return to God's presence without them."[56]

History of LDS Temples

Mormons believe that God ordered them to build temples. They built their first temple in Kirkland, Ohio, in 1836. Joseph Smith claimed that it was God's instruction to build the temple, and though it was a financial hardship, the faithful built the temple. Mormons used this first temple in a different way than subsequent temples. When God first gave this instruction to Joseph Smith, the temple they built in Kirkland was more like what they call a tabernacle now. They used it for worship and for regular church meetings. The Temple ordinances did not come until later. By the time they built the second temple in Nauvoo, Illinois, Mormon doctrine had developed, and the Nauvoo temple had many of the characteristics of today's temples.

Once Mormons established their presence in the Salt Lake Valley, work began on the Salt Lake Temple. Forty years in the building and dedicated in 1893, it is the best known of the temples. In the time it took to build, the saints built a temple in three other Utah cities: St. George, Logan, and Manti.

Mormons believe that their temples are in the tradition of the temple of the Old Testament. They trace their belief in temples from the tabernacle Moses constructed during the Exodus, through the temples of Solomon, Zerubbabel, and

Herod. For our Mormon friend, today's temples are similar in form and function to those ancient ones.

Mormons believe that Judaism is a branch of Christianity. They believe the church goes all the way back to Adam, who was a prophet of the church just as the current prophet in Salt Lake City is now. In this vein, they believe that the activities in today's LDS temples are the same activities carried out by all the prophets, beginning with Adam. These activities, Mormons call them sacred ordinances, are of highest importance and critical to a person's acceptance into the celestial kingdom. (See Appendix VII)

Purpose of Temples

Because the temple is off limits to non-Mormons and LDS authorities command members not to speak about what happens there, a lot of speculation remains about what does happen in a temple. I have determined to talk only about those things LDS authors have revealed in their own writings. My sources for this discussion include no references to non-Mormon authors or works.

Before LDS young people leave for their mission, or before they are married, they begin going to the temple. First they receive their "endowments." These endowments, they believe, "are necessary for you, after you have departed this life, to enable you to walk back to the presence of the Father, passing the angels who stand as sentinels . . . and gain your eternal exaltation."[57] The endowment ceremony is a melodrama that explains the creation and the fall. It is in this ceremony that they receive the authority or the privilege of being in the priesthood of the LDS Church.

One of the things we will hear about our Mormon friend or neighbor is that they wear special underwear. They will not be open to talking to us about this. The wearing of "garments," as they call them, is one of those sacred items not to be discussed outside the temple, especially with nonmembers. As a part of receiving the endowments, LDS members make a covenant to endure to the end, as the Savior endured to the end. They believe they demonstrate this commitment by wearing a special garment that demonstrates enduring faith in Him and in His eternal covenants with the member.

LDS people are encouraged to wear this garment as underclothing both day and night. They are told not to remove it unless absolutely necessary, such as for swimming or bathing, but then it should be restored as soon as possible. "Endowed members of the Church wear the garment as a reminder of the sacred covenants they have made with the Lord and also as a protection against temptation and evil. How it is worn is an outward expression of an inward commitment to follow the Savior."[58]

Mormons believe the temple is the place on earth where the veil between heaven and earth is the thinnest. It is almost heaven. It is in this place, so close to heaven itself, that some ordinances are done in proxy for persons in the past who died without the opportunity to do them for themselves. Mormons trace genealogies to discover the names of people who died without having an opportunity to hear the restored gospel. These people, who have been resurrected because of the atonement of Jesus, are stuck in the place of the resurrected dead. They are waiting for a present day Mormon to be baptized in their place. When that happens, the deceased and resurrected person receives the opportunity to accept the gospel of Mormonism. Until this proxy baptism takes place, they have no opportunity for heaven.

One of the purposes of the temple is Temple Marriage. Mormons believe that a regular marriage, one performed outside the temple, is a marriage for time only. That is why the standard wedding ceremony states "until death do us part." However, weddings performed in the temple are for all time and eternity. By the authority of the Priesthood they are sealed as husband and wife to one another. This sealing authority is effective past the grave.

When children are added to these eternal marriages, the children are sealed to their parents, thus they remain a family forever. The LDS advertising slogan, "Families are Forever" is a reference to this ordinance. Eternal marriage is very important, not just for the marriage and the eternal family, for unless one is married in this eternal fashion, he or she is unable to enter into the highest celestial glory. (See Appendix VII)

Each temple has a Celestial room. Located on the top floor of the temple, the room is furnished with fine chairs, sofas, tables, lamps, etc. This room is for the member to sit in and contemplate heaven. The celestial room is as close to heaven as one can get on earth. Since it is so close to the separating veil and the veil is especially thin here, it is almost like being in heaven. A person can't get any closer to heaven than this room until he or she dies.

Worthiness

We may have heard the term "temple Mormon" or perhaps "temple worthy" in our discussion about Mormonism. There are very strict regulations concerning who may enter into a temple and receive endowments, enjoy a celestial marriage, or just do their temple proxy work. The temple ordinances and ceremonies are so sacred they are not to be talked about among the unprepared. Of course, the first step in preparation is to be or become a member of the Church of Jesus Christ of Latter-day Saints. This includes the preliminary steps of faith, repentance, baptism, confirmation, and membership in the church. Any person desiring to enter a temple must have a worthiness and a maturity to come as a guest to the house of the Lord.

An interview with a bishop determines one's dignity and worthiness. According to a LDS church booklet about temples, "Worthiness is determined by a bishop interview. The bishop will make inquiry into your personal worthiness. He will ask searching questions. The candidate must certify that he or she is morally clean and is keeping the Word of Wisdom, paying a full tithing, living in harmony with the teachings of the church, and not maintaining any affiliation or sympathy with apostate groups."[59] If the Bishop finds the candidate worthy of the temple, he issues a temple recommend. After another interview by the stake president, the LDS member can then attend the temple.

Other Ordinances

Mormons have two ordinances that do not require the temple, and both are very similar to the ordinances in evangelical churches. The first of these is baptism. Mormons practice baptism by total immersion. They believe that baptism is a necessary part of salvation. Before one can become a member of the LDS church, a person must be baptized. It is valid only if a member of the LDS priesthood performs it. The person doing the baptism must recite the exact words of the baptism ordinance with another person in authority checking. If the watching authority does not confirm the use of the exact words, the baptism must be repeated.

Mormons do not baptize infants. Children are eligible for baptism when they reach the age of accountability, which the LDS church has determined to be eight years old. Soon after a child's eighth birthday, he or she will undergo the rite of baptism. If Evangelicals are living in a community where there is a significant LDS population, it is likely their third grade children will begin to ask about baptism because all of their LDS friends are proudly talking about their baptism.

Every week in the Sacrament meeting, the ward or congregation observes the other ordinance, the sacrament. It is similar to what others call communion or the Lord's Supper. They use store bought white bread straight from the package. The deacons tear the bread into pieces and distribute it with plain water as the fruit of the vine. There is no effort to maintain Jesus' symbolism of the unleavened bread and the blood of Christ.

Serving deacons are twelve and thirteen year old boys in the LDS church. One of the serving deacons blesses the sacrament. After he says the prescribed blessing and gets the okay that he said the words correctly, adding none nor leaving any out, the boys pass out the bread and water. As each recipient receives his or her portion, he or she eats and drinks. There is neither further ceremony nor explanation of its meaning. There is no mention of it representing the blood and body of the Lord Jesus. Taking this sacrament on a weekly basis is fundamental to keeping the covenant made with the Lord at baptism. Partaking of this sacrament renews the covenants and keeps them current for the LDS church member.

What About Temples?

That other faith systems don't have temples, or an interest in temples, is as incredible to the LDS faithful as their having the temples is mysterious to evangelicals. A difference in the meaning of religion itself accounts for this.

Mormons believe "that God has one Plan of Salvation and one Church, and that it was the same Church that was given to Adam and all of the prophets in the Old Testament; it was the same Church that Jesus Christ established and clarified and corrected when he was on earth; it was the same Church presided over by Paul and the Apostles until they were all killed or died; and it's the same Church that was restored by Joseph Smith."[60]

Their understanding is that the Jewish temples of the Old Testament were for the same "Christian" function for which Mormons use temples today. Evangelicals and other Christians believe this is far from the truth. The Old Testament explains the function of the tabernacle in the wilderness and later the temples of Judaism.

The tabernacle/temple was a place of sacrifice. Jews did not use their temples for weddings. Nobody was ever sealed to anybody in the temple. Baptisms did not take place in the temple. Those were not the uses of the temple. The temple was a place where a priest offered sacrifice for the sins of the people. The Old Testament book of Leviticus gives explicit instructions and explanations for these sacrifices. The priest offered the Trespass, Sin, Peace, and Meal Offerings before God. These offerings pointed to a new covenant, one to be fulfilled in Jesus Christ.

Hebrews chapter 9 explains this. All of those offerings happened daily for hundreds of years. Over and over the offering of the sacrifice pointed to one sacrifice, one offering. When Jesus

Christ died on the cross, His sacrifice made one final payment for sin. This sacrifice was sufficient for all time. The New Testament account of the crucifixion uses this as proof. When Jesus died on the cross, he was the ultimate, final sacrifice.

In the Temple there was a veil that separated the holy place from the Holy of Holies. The Holy of Holies was the place where God dwelled. According to the Gospels, when Jesus died on the cross, that veil was miraculously torn in half from top to bottom. Just before Jesus died, he said, "It is finished. " The meaning of the word is translated "paid in full." When Jesus Christ gave himself on the cross, he became the final sacrifice, and the need for a temple was over. There was a new covenant. The people now lived in a new era. Soon the Holy Spirit would come, and the dwelling place of God would be the human heart, not a building made with hands (See Acts 17:24).

Conclusion

The sacrifice of Jesus on the Cross was the final payment for sin. Since sacrifice was the purpose for the temple, the need for a temple came to an end. Jesus was the fulfillment of the temple.

The temple plays a large part in LDS theology. It is the location for the mystical and mysterious endowments. Mormon children continually hear of the holiness and importance of the temple. and they hold their temple buildings in awe. Our LDS neighbors are proud of the beautiful temples of the church and will probably be able to tell many stories of their effectiveness. While the temple plays a large role in LDS theology, it has no place in Christian theology.

9

The Priesthood

Where Do You Get Your Authority?

For our LDS friends, their Priesthood is one of the key factors that makes them the only true church. The Priesthood gives them the authority to act on behalf of God. Their understanding of priesthood is unique. They stress the importance and benefits of the priesthood so highly our Mormon friend will have trouble understanding how we can even have a church when we do not have the priesthood authority that God reestablished through Joseph Smith. This part of Mormonism is difficult for a non-Mormon to comprehend. To Mormons, the concept of priesthood is one of the more critical elements of their religion, yet it is almost non-existent in Evangelicalism.

One of the ways Mormons believe God restored the church was a restoration of the priesthood. One day in 1829, in either April or May, depending on which source of Joseph's testimony is used, Joseph Smith and Oliver Cowdery were in the woods when a messenger of the Lord conferred the Aaronic priesthood on them. Sometime later they met with some of Jesus' first century apostles, and the apostles ordained them to the Melchizedek priesthood. This priesthood gives them the authority to be the true church of Jesus Christ. Only the LDS church has this priesthood authority.

The blessing of the priesthood gives an LDS man authority to act for God. Without that authority, the non-LDS among us are powerless to carry on the ordinances of the church. All other churches on the face of the earth are false since only the LDS church has this restored priesthood. Faithful men who are members of the LDS Church have the opportunity to receive two different priesthoods. Both priesthoods have a succession of offices to advance through. The Aaronic Priesthood is the lesser priesthood. Boys receive this priesthood when they reach the age of 12. The higher priesthood is the Melchizedek Priesthood, which is reserved to the age of 18 (for a list of the offices in each priesthood see Appendix III).

The LDS definition of priesthood is "the authority to act in the name of God." Therefore, for a church to function, the followers have to have the authority to act on God's behalf, and they can only do that with the priesthood. The priesthood confers that authority on the people who hold it. The priesthood is handed down from one priest to another. There is a succession to this authority. It all proceeds from the priesthood authority given to Joseph Smith and Oliver Cowdery by Peter, James, and John in 1829. God uses this authority to govern, sustain, create, redeem, and exalt the whole human family.

Our Mormon friend believes that unless a man holds the priesthood, he has no authority to perform the ordinances of the church, so the LDS church ordinances are the only ordinances that have any meaning to God because only the LDS church has the priesthood. All of the servings and callings in the church are performed by the authorization of the priesthood. The importance of this priesthood in Mormonism cannot be over emphasized.

The LDS teaching is that God gave Adam the priesthood. Adam was the first priest, and the priesthood was passed down, beginning from Adam until the day of Moses. When the people rebelled in the desert during the Exodus, God removed the Melchizedek priesthood from them. They justify this by using Joseph Smith's inspired version of the Bible. Neither the Hebrew text nor the English translations of that text say anything about God removing a priesthood.

Mormons teach that this was the reason God established the lesser, or the Aaronic, priesthood. Since it is a lesser priesthood, a man who holds this priesthood has authority to act as a legal administrator of God in certain ways. He has the authority to preach the gospel of repentance. He has the authority to baptize and to administer the sacrament. A priest can lead meetings, be involved in the basic teaching programs of the church, be a home visitor, and participate in the missionary work of the Church. This is the only priesthood that was on the earth from Moses until John the Baptist. John the Baptist was the last one to hold the Aaronic priesthood until it was restored in these latter days.

The Melchizedek Priesthood is the authority that operates The Church of Jesus Christ of Latter-day Saints. This Melchizedek Priesthood holds the right of presidency and has power and authority over all the offices in the church in all ages of the world, to administer in spiritual things. The power and authority of the higher priesthood, the Melchizedek Priesthood, is to hold the keys of all the spiritual blessings of the church. Without the Melchizedek Priesthood, there is no authority to be a church, no authority to enjoy the presence of God the Father, and no communion with Jesus.

This is the teaching of the LDS church that leads to their exclusivity. They teach that they have the exclusive authority to be a church, to baptize, to teach, to evangelize. They believe it is only through their church that anyone will ever get to the highest heaven. Our friends or neighbors may not believe this totally, but if they accept their church's teaching, they think that we have nothing spiritual if we are not a Mormon.

The Biblical Belief Concerning Priesthood

What does the Bible say about priests, priesthoods, and Melchizedek in particular? Before we talk about the use of the priesthood, we need to understand this doctrine of Melchizedek. The Bible mentions Melchizedek in three places: Genesis 14, Psalm 110, and Hebrews 5 - 7. In Genesis, Abraham and his allies are returning from a victorious battle when they reach the King's Valley. The King of Sodom and the King of Salem come to meet Abraham. Salem was the early name for what later became Jerusalem. Genesis says that the name of the king of Salem was Melchizedek and that he was a priest of God Most High. He blessed Abraham, and Abraham gave him a tithe of the spoils. That is all that exists in the historical record about Melchizedek or his priesthood. There is no mention of Melchizedek or the Melchizedek priesthood throughout the history of the Hebrews.

In the non-historical book of Psalms there is a reference to a coming Messiah. Psalm 110 is called a Messianic psalm, a prophetic psalm about the coming messiah. The Psalmist says the messiah will be a priest according to the order of Melchizedek, or a priest like Melchizedek. That is all it says. There is no explanation. The coming messiah will be a priest like Melchizedek, and he will be a priest forever.

The third reference to Melchizedek is in the New Testament book of Hebrews and brings clarity to the issue. The writer of Hebrews is talking about the superiority of Jesus Christ, and he makes five arguments. The first is that Jesus is greater than the angels. Second, Jesus is greater than Moses. Then, He is greater than the Old Testament priesthood. Fourth, the New Covenant is superior to the old Covenant, and fifth, it is all received by faith.

The third declaration could be a problem for a Jewish believer. Jesus was not a Levite, and in Judaism, only the Levites could be priests. The writer talks about Jesus being a priest, but a Jew would know that Jesus was from the tribe of Judah, not Levi. Judah was the tribe of kings, not priests. The kings all came from Judah. The priests all came from Levi. The kings were descendants of David; the priests of Moses. Jesus was a descendant of David. Hebrews explains it like this. Jesus is a priest like Melchizedek was a priest. Melchizedek was a priest before there was a Levitical priesthood. Jesus is a priest like that. Like Melchizedek, Jesus remains the priest forever. He is the high priest. He is the one with authority. He is the mediator between God and man. Jesus holds the office forever. That is why Evangelicals don't have priests. Jesus is our high priest. We have authority as his children to act on his behalf. We are his body on the earth. We make intercession on his behalf; we are his ambassadors, as if God were appealing to the world through us (2 Corinthians 5:17).

Conclusion

The doctrine of the priesthood answers the question, "Where do you get your authority?" Our Mormon friend believes his authority comes from his church, through the priesthood restored to Joseph Smith in 1829 and passed down through the LDS church. Evangelical Christians believe our authority comes by virtue of the fact that we are the children of God. "To as many as received him, to them he gave the authority to be the children of God" (John 1:12). Our authority is Jesus' authority.

Appendix I

A Short history of Mormonism

Joseph Smith organized his church in 1830 in New York. The name of the church became the Church of Jesus Christ of Latter-day Saints. He established the church with a story of dreams and visions. He told of a visit to his room by an angel named Moroni who told him of a book written on golden plates buried in the ground not far from him. The book was an account of the former inhabitants of the continent.

According to Smith, after several visits from the angel and a yearly visit to the site for four years, the messenger allowed him to retrieve the plates and begin to translate them with the help of two seer stones. They told the story of the American continent and the visit of Jesus Christ to the Americas after his ascension in Jerusalem.

The translated plates became the Book of Mormon, from which the Mormon church gets the name by which many call them. Early Mormon belief included the building of a new Zion. The Mormons began the building of their new Zion in Kirtland, Ohio, in 1831. There they built their homes and farms and established their first Temple. When they were forced to leave Ohio, Joseph Smith located the new Zion in Jackson county, Missouri.

Every history has facts and interpretation of facts. Mormons tell their history as a series of persecutions that eventually drove them to the Mountain West and the valley of the Great Salt Lake. Their opponents in each place tell of Mormon indiscretions. In Ohio they began to have some financial problems. Smith applied for a charter to begin a bank, and when the state turned down his application, he established an "anti-bank" instead. He printed and issued the Church's own currency, and they tried to pay their debts with it. When the local authorities issued an arrest warrant for banking fraud, Joseph Smith slipped out of Ohio in the middle of the night. Mormon historian Richard Van Wagoner says, "Kirtland Saints were not driven from the land by malevolent vigilantes. They voluntarily sought sanctuary in Missouri to dwell with their expatriate prophet and his spokesman, who had fled Kirtland in early 1838 to elude creditors and probable imprisonment."[61]

They prospered for a while in Jackson County, Missouri. Depending on which version one believes, they were either pushed out because of their political power or they were pushed out because of their theology. Their political power came because they tended to vote in a block, thus multiplying their power. They were also mostly anti-slavery and thus drew the opposition of the slave holders. Theologically, they taught that Jackson County was the land of Zion that God had given to the Mormons. Non-Mormons were intruders upon the land and should be removed. In the ensuing conflict, the Mormons were driven north and settled in Caldwell County, Missouri.

Eventually similar conflicts arose, only this time they deteriorated into a shooting war. The Mormons were finally run out of Missouri, so they settled in Illinois. Whether it was political or religious, troubles came again. This time the main trouble came from inside the church. It was becoming impossible to keep the practice of polygamy secret any longer. Joseph Smith, his brother Hyrum, and all of the twelve apostles were taking multiple wives. Mormons opposed to polygamy left the church, and one of them began a newspaper. The first edition of the Nauvoo Expositor exposed the practice of polygamy. After that edition, on the orders of Mayor Joseph Smith, the city prosecutor, Hyrum Smith, who was Joseph Smith's brother, destroyed the Expositor's presses in the middle of the night.

This episode was the reason for Smith's arrest. Illinois authorities put Joseph and Hyrum in jail in Carthage. There was also an arrest warrant for Smith in Missouri, and depending on which story one accepts, a force from Missouri was either coming to extradite Joseph back to Missouri for trial or they were coming to lynch him. A troop of Missourians did come to Carthage. Mormons teach that it was to lynch Joseph and that he was lynched by the mob. The Missourians claimed Smith was killed while trying to escape. Joseph and Hyrum had weapons that had been smuggled to them, and when the Missourians approached, they began firing. Mormons say that Joseph Smith was a martyr, but in his martyrdom, he killed two Missourians and wounded another.

Brigham Young became the new leader and led the people to the Valley of the Great Salt Lake. The stories of the journey are truly heroic. The history of the Mormon settlements in Utah is a tribute to their industry and Young's leadership. Once in Salt Lake City, the Mormons set about to colonize the whole region. They sent settlers into all parts of Utah and into the surrounding states. Other Mormons continued down the trail to California. Many Utah families can trace their family's arrival in Utah to their ancestors who made these early journeys. They are justifiably proud of their history.

Appendix II

Requirements for Exaltation

The time to fulfill the requirements for exaltation is now (see Alma 34:32-34). President Joseph Fielding Smith said, "In order to obtain the exaltation we must accept the gospel and all its covenants; and take upon us the obligations which the Lord has offered; and walk in the light and understanding of the truth; and live by every word that proceedeth forth from the mouth of God'" (Doctrines of Salvation, 2:43).

To be exalted, we first must place our faith in Jesus Christ and then endure in that faith to the end of our lives. Our faith in him must be such that we repent of our sins and obey his commandments.

He commands us all to receive certain ordinances:

1. We must be baptized and confirmed a member of the Church of Jesus Christ.

2. We must receive the laying on of hands for the gift of the Holy Ghost.

3. We must receive the temple endowment.

4. We must be married for time and eternity.

In addition to receiving the required ordinances, the Lord commands all of us to –

1. Love and worship God.

2. Love our neighbor.

3. Repent of our wrongdoings.

4. Live the law of chastity.

5. Pay honest tithes and offerings.

6. Be honest in our dealings with others and with the Lord.

7. Speak the truth always.

8. Obey the Word of Wisdom.

9. Search out our kindred dead and perform the saving ordinances of the gospel for them.

10. Keep the Sabbath day holy.

11. Attend our Church meetings as regularly as possible so we can renew our baptismal covenants by partaking of the sacrament.

12. Love our family members and strengthen them in the ways of the Lord.

13. Have family and individual prayers every day.

14. Honor our parents.

15. Teach the gospel to others by word and example.

16. Study the scriptures.

17. Listen to and obey the inspired words of the prophets of the Lord.

Finally, each of us needs to receive the Holy Ghost and learn to follow his direction in our individual lives.

Source: *Gospel Principles.* Published by the Church of Jesus Christ of Latter-day Saints, Salt Lake City, Utah, 1997, pp. 303-304.

Appendix III

The Organization of the Church

The LDS Church has the same offices as the ancient church. It includes Apostles, prophets, seventies, evangelists (patriarchs), pastors (presiding officers), high priests, elders, bishops, priests, teachers, and deacons.

A prophet, acting under the direction of the Lord, leads the church as president.

Two counselors assist the President.

Twelve apostles are responsible for the work of the church worldwide.

Other general officers of the Church with special assignments include the Presiding Bishopric and the Quorums of the Seventy.

The LDS church is organized and led by the priesthood. The Priesthood has two parts. The Melchizedek or greater priesthood, and the Aaronic or lesser priesthood.

Aaronic Priesthood Offices.

Deacon: 12-13 year old boys

Teacher: 14-15 year old boys

Priest: 16-17 year old boys.

Bishop: Presides over the Aaronic Priesthood and also holds the Melchizedek Priesthood office of High priest.

Melchizedek Priesthood Offices

Elder: teach, expound, exhort, baptize, and watch over the church.

High Priest: Officiate the church. Stake presidents, mission presidents, high councilors, bishoprics

Patriarch: Give blessings

Seventy: Assist in building up and regulating the Church.

Apostle: members of the Quorum of Twelve Apostles. The senior Apostle is president of the church.

Source: *Gospel Principles.* Published by the Church of Jesus Christ of Latter-day Saints, Salt Lake City, Utah, 1997, p. 112.

APPENDIX IV

The Adam God Doctrine

I am not going to detail the doctrine here. There are plenty of sources available for that. Since none of our friends believe it, it is not part of the subject of this book. However, the way we differ in our understanding of revelation is pertinent to the book, and it is on display in this doctrine.

The confusion that afflicts the serious student of Mormonism is understanding the prophetic authority of the church. When is a prophet a prophet and when is he not? When does he speak with authority and when does he speak for himself? Do the prophets speak with revelation authority? Even the LDS prophets and apostles don't agree among themselves.

This lack of clarity makes Mormon doctrine difficult to understand. LDS authorities do not agree on what their authority is. For example, former LDS president Ezra Taft Benson in the *Life and Teachings of Ezra Taft Benson* says the teachings of the current president prophet have the authority of scripture. "What the prophet says is scripture," Benson further says the teachings in his book ought to be scripture. Joseph Smith and Brigham Young both said that when the prophet speaks, it is scripture.

Modern BYU professors, and those like the apostle I interviewed, say that they do not have that authority unless they are sustained by the church.

There is difficulty determining which is the right belief. Which do we believe? How do we know? It appears to us that our LDS friends do not have any standard by which to say, "This is what we believe." If we show them an authentic quote from Brigham Young's teaching, they are liable to just say, "We don't believe that." We may think, "But he is a prophet. He taught that as a prophet." Their response remains, "That doesn't make any difference; we don't believe that."

Steven Robinson, professor of ancient scripture at Brigham Young University, says this.

> The latter-day Saints have never believed that Brigham Young taught the Adam God theory, as explained in anti-Mormon literature, and that whether Brigham Young believed it or not, the Adam God theory as proposed and interpreted by non-Mormons simply cannot be found in the theology of the LDS Saints. I do not believe it; my parents do not believe it; and neither did their parents before them. Yet there are few anti-Mormon publications that do not present this Adam God theory, the doctrinal creation of our opponents as one of the most characteristic doctrines of the Latter Day Saints. This is certainly misrepresentation; I believe it is also dishonest.

I don't think we understand one another. They don't believe the Adam God theory. Our neighbors don't believe that. They insist that it is not part of their theology, and we must accept that. They don't teach it: they don't believe it. That is fair, but it is disingenuous of them to say that Brigham Young didn't teach it. He did. He taught it over a period of twenty years.

The relevant question here is not what they believe about Adam God. The question is about revelation. How do they decide what to believe? This was the basis for the question I asked LDS Apostle Neil Maxwell. Can a prophet teach something that is wrong?

He refused to answer my question, and with good reason. If he said "no," then anyone could produce these teachings of Brigham Young that Adam is the God of this world and ask, "Then what about this doctrine?" If he said "yes," they could teach something that is wrong, and then of course the question becomes, "Then how do you know that he is correct any other time?" This would include all of their extra biblical scripture.

If Joseph Smith was wrong about the book of Abraham, how can a Mormon believe what he said about the Book of Mormon? If he couldn't translate the Egyptian manuscripts that we have copies of correctly, how do Latter Day Saints know he translated the ones we don't have correctly? This kind of thinking reflects the evangelical worldview. Our Mormon friends don't have that problem because they believe that revelation is open, flexible, and expanding. They believes the prophet is right, because he is the prophet. Even if he is wrong, he can't be wrong.

This continues to be our handicap as we try to compare their doctrine to ours. Understanding LDS doctrine is difficult. I suspect it is just as difficult for them to understand our doctrine because we simply do not agree on the very basic nature of revelation.

Appendix V

The Joseph Smith Translation of the Bible

During his lifetime Joseph Smith made 3410 changes to the King James Version of the Bible. He claimed that these changes were made at the direction of the Lord although he had no Greek or Hebrew manuscript evidence. These changes were made by direct revelation to the prophet.

Another early Mormon, former Reformed Baptist and Campbellite preacher Sidney Rigdon, was also instrumental in the new translation. There is some dispute among LDS scholars as to how large a role Rigdon played. LDS scholar Richard S. Van Wagoner in his book about Rigdon claims that after Joseph Smith died, his wife Emma offered the original manuscript of the retranslation to him. (Sidney Rigdon, *A Portrait of Religious Excess*, Signature Books, Salt Lake City. p. 437.)

The church has published this translation, and it is available for purchase. In the current King James Bible published by the LDS church, there are references and notes referring to the JST (Joseph Smith Translation).

Appendix VI

Mormons and polygamy

The strange Mormon doctrine that probably gets the most attention is one they don't hold anymore. Polygamy is a part of Mormonism's past, but the current Mormon Church is emphatically against the practice. They claim they will excommunicate anyone who practices it.

Joseph Smith began practicing polygamy secretly as early as 1831. He revealed it to only a few people until he was required to instruct the leading priesthood brethren in 1841. In 1843 he dictated the revelation to William Clayton.

By the time of his death, Joseph, Hyrum, and all twelve of the apostles were practicing plural marriage. The practice was one of the major reasons the Mormons lost the favor of the people of Illinois. It was an issue of the *Nauvoo Expositor* exposing the practice that caused Hyrum, under Joseph's orders, to destroy their presses. Joseph and Hyrum were arrested, and after that they were killed at the Carthage jail.

In Utah in 1852, church leaders announced to the church in a special conference that the church was practicing plural marriage. This practice continued until 1890 when President Wilford Woodruff issued Official Declaration 1.

The history of Utah over the next years is an interesting story of arrests, secret marriages, and intrigue, but eventually polygamy lost out. The fundamental Mormon Polygamist groups that exist today claim the Official Declaration was a political cave to the U.S. government and that the real church of Jesus Christ practices polygamy. Polygamists remain a force in Utah today. It doesn't take much sleuthing to discover the polygamist communities scattered around the state. Utah law enforcers leave them alone unless other crimes are being committed and someone makes a complaint.

They believe that the limit of one wife is an earthly limit; however, in the celestial kingdom, God's people will once again practice celestial marriage.

Source: David J. Ridges, *Mormon Beliefs and Doctrines Mad Easier* (Springville, Utah: Cedar Fort, Inc., 2007), 242-3.

Appendix VII

The Mormon View of Heaven

The LDS church teaching regarding heaven is different than the orthodox Christian view. They begin by defining 3 different realms of glory. There are the Telestial, Terrestrial, and Celestial Kingdoms. In addition there is a fourth possible eternal destination for humans. They are clear that it is not a form of glory, rather it is Perdition, or the outer darkness.

Perdition is reserved for Satan and his followers. They will be joined there by those humans who are resurrected and found unworthy of any kingdom of glory. These are the people who know the truth and then willingly choose to sin against the truth. "Their sin is unpardonable. These are cast into the outer darkness. (D&C 76:31-39,44-48.)" [1]

The Telestial Kingdom is reserved for those who on the final Judgment Day are still "liars, and sorcerers, and adulterers, and whoremongers, and whosoever loves and makes a lie" (D&C 76:103).[2]

The Terrestrial Kingdom is for good and honorable people but who choose not to become valiant and faithful members of the Lord's Church despite having a fair opportunity to do so.[3]

Celestial Glory is heaven. This is reserved for members of the LDS church who follow the church's doctrines. There are three degrees within the Celestial Kingdom. The highest of these is exaltation. "Exaltation is the type of life that Heavenly Father lives. Celestial marriage is a requirement for exaltation (D&C

---

[1] Robert Millet, *The Mormon Faith; A New Look at Christianity* (Salt Lake City: Shadow Mountain, 1998), 68.

[2] David J. Ridges, *Mormon Beliefs and Doctrines Mad Easier* (Springville: Cedar Fort, Inc. 2007), 160.

[3] Ibid.

132:19-20). Husbands and wives who attain exaltation will become gods, have spirit children, make worlds for them, and send them through the same plan of salvation used for us by the Father (First Presidency statement, *Improvement Era,* D&C 105:32). [4]

---

[4] Ridges, 161.

ENDNOTES

[1] B. H. Roberts, *The Mormon Doctrine of Deity* (Salt Lake City: Signature Books, 1903, reprint 1998), 86.

[2] Robert Millet, *The Mormon Faith; A New Look at Christianity* (Salt Lake City: Shadow Mountain, 1998), 187.

[3] *Gospel Principles* (Salt Lake City: The Church of Jesus Christ of Latter Day Saints, 1997), 52.

[4] Ibid., 55.

[5] Millet, 14.

[6] Dallin Oaks, "Scripture Reading and Revelation," *Ensign*, January 1995.

[7] Neil Maxwell, Personal interview on January 21, 2003, Salt Lake City.

[8] Millet, 17.

[9] Ibid.. 24.

[10] Ibid.

[11] Bruce R. McConkie, *Mormon Doctrine* (Salt Lake City: Publishers Press, 1966), 82.

[12] Gleason Archer, *A Survey of Old Testament Introduction* (Chicago: Moody Press, 1985), 513-517.

[13] W. F. Walker Johanson, *What is Mormonism All About? Answers to the 150 Most Commonly Asked Questions About The Church of Jesus Christ of Latter-day Saints* (New York: St. Martin's Griffin, 2002),17.

[14] History of the Church, 4:461 as quoted in *Gospel Principles*, 53.

[15] Johanson, 23.

[16] Ibid.

[17] Ibid.

[18] Explanatory Introduction to *The Doctrine and Covenants*.

[19] *Gospel Principles*, 54.

[20] Ibid.

[21] McConkie, 564.

[22] Millet, Appendix.
[23] Millet, 29.
[24] David J. Ridges, *Mormon Beliefs and Doctrines Mad Easier* (Springville: Cedar Fort, Inc. 2007), 119.
[25] Millet, 187.
[26] Daniel H. Ludlow, ed., *Jesus Christ and His Gospel; Selections from the Encyclopedia of Mormonism* (Salt Lake City: Deseret Book, 1992), 192.
[27] Joseph Smith, as quoted in Ludlow, 193.
[28] Ridges, 122.
[29] Millet, 28-29.
[30] Gordon B. Hinckley, "We Testify of Jesus Christ," *Ensign*, March 2008, 7.
[31] Ludlow, 255.
[32] In LDS terms the word is Jehovah. That is the way it is used in the King James Bible. More recently scholars believe the correct translation of the word would be Yahweh. Either way, they translate the same Hebrew word. In this work I will use the word Jehovah for consistency.
[33] Ludlow, 252.

[34] McConkie, 742.
[35] Ludlow, 256-7.
[36] Ibid., 256.
[37] Millet, 169.
[38] Ibid.
[39] Johanson, 153.
[40] Ibid., 165.
[41] *Gospel Principles*, 75.
[42] Lloyd R. Scott, "Elder M. Russell Ballard Outlines Gospel Principles," *Deseret News*, Salt Lake City, November 7, 2010.
[43] Ludlow, 124-125
[44] Jeffrey R. Holland, "The Atonement of Jesus Christ," *Ensign*, March 2008, Vol. 38, Number 3, 35.
[45] Ludlow, 154.

[46] Ibid., 384.
[47] Ibid., 208.
[48] http://www.sfgate.com/news/article/SUNDAY-INTERVIEW-Musings-of-the-Main-Mormon-2846138.php
[49] "Kingdom Come," *Time*, August 4, 1997, p. 56
[50] https://www.lds.org/general-conference/1997/10/drawing-nearer-to-the-lord?lang=eng
[51] *Gospel Principles*, 302.
[52] *Gospel Principles*, 303.
[53] *Gospel Principles*, 305.
[54] Millet,175.
[55] LeGrand Richards, *A Marvelous Work and a Wonder* (Whitefish: Kessinger Publishing, 2004), 357.
[56] Howard W. Hunter, "A Temple-Motivated People," in *Temples of the Church of Jesus Christ of Latter-Day Saints* (Salt Lake City: Church of Jesus Christ of Latter Day Saints, 2010), 38.
[57] Russell M. Nelson, "Prepare for the Blessings of the Temple," *Temples of the Church of Jesus Christ of Latter-Day Saints* (Salt Lake City: Church of Jesus Christ of Latter Day Saints, 2010), 42.
[58] Nelson, 47.
[59] Boyd K. Packer, "The Holy Temple," *Temples of the Church of Jesus Christ of Latter-Day Saints* (Salt Lake City: Church of Jesus Christ of Latter Day Saints, 2010), 30-31.
[60] Johanson, 132.
[61] Richard S. Van Wagoner, *Sidney Rigdon, A portrait of Religious Excess* (Salt Lake City: Signature Books,1994), 117.

Made in the USA
San Bernardino, CA
29 July 2015